Start Your Own

FOOD TRUCK BUSINESS

Additional titles in *Entrepreneur's Startup Series*

Start Your Own

Entrepreneur MAGAZINE'S

startup

Start Your Own

FOOD TRUCK BUSINESS

Cart ◆ Trailer ◆ Kiosk

Standard and Gourmet Trucks

Mobile Catering ◆ Bustaurant

Entrebreneur Press and Rich Mintzer

EP
Entrepreneur
Press

Jere L. Calmes, Publisher
Managing Editor: Marla Markman
Cover Design: Beth Hansen-Winter
Production and Composition: Eliot House Productions

This publication is designed to provide accurate and authoritative information in regard to the subject matter covered. It is sold with the understanding that the publisher is not engaged in rendering legal, accounting or other professional services. If legal advice or other expert assistance is required, the services of a competent professional person should be sought.

Library of Congress Cataloging-in-Publication Data
    Start your own food truck business/by Entrepreneur Press and Rich Mintzer.
      p.   cm.
    ISBN-10: 1-59918-414-1 (pbk.)
    ISBN-13: 978-1-59918-414-2 (pbk.)
      1. Food industry and trade—United States—Management. 2. Food service—United States—Management. 3. New business enterprises—United States. I. Mintzer, Richard. II. Entrepreneur Press.
    HD9005.S73 2011
    647.95—dc22   2011004512

Printed in the United States of America

15 14 13 12 11   10 9 8 7 6 5 4 3 2 1

Contents

Chapter 4

What's Off the Menu? **43**

Chapter 5

Can I Park Here?
Licenses, Regulations, and Points of Sales **59**

Chapter 6

The Work Environment: Commercial Kitchens,
Cleaning, and Hiring Help **73**

▲

▲

Acknowledgments

I'd like to thank Jere Calmes for the opportunity to write this book. It was great fun to write largely because of the input from so many helpful individuals who take great pride in their work.

I'd also like to thank Zach Brooks, founder and owner, Midtownlunch.com; Natasha Usher from Lucinda Creperie, Jersey City, NJ; Laura O'Neill, Van Leeuwen Artisan Ice Cream; Cody and Kristen Fields, Mmmpanadas, Austin, TX; Michelle Lozuaway and Josh Lanahan, Fresh Local, Portsmouth, NH; Scott Baitinger and Steve Mai, Streetza, Milwaukee; Adria Shimada, Parfait Ice Cream,

Seattle; Phil and Deb Anson and Danielle Winslow, EVOL Foods , Boulder, CO (and thank you for the boxes of burritos—yum!!); Celine Legros of Les Caneies de Celine, New York (also thanks for the great sample pastries); Chef Biagio Barone and Deborah Hertlein, GotChef, Milford, CT; Joe Rubin, FundingPost (and GotChef) Milford, CT; Mike Boyd, Cart King; Robert Smith, All Star Carts & Kiosks; Kris Ruby, The Ruby Media Group LLC, Westchester, NY; Laura Katen, Katen Consulting, Westchester, NY; Mark Sampson, CrowdSpring.com; Eric Stite, founder and president, Franchise Business Review; Cheryl Kimball who's always a great help; and Tom Guiltinan, Nancy Biberman, Marcus Gotay, Kerry McLean, Khushbu Srivastava, and Rebecca Koopman, all of whom were terrific hosts at WHEDco where they walked me through their fabulous commercial kitchens in the Bronx. Thank you all very much.

Preface

If you enjoy cooking, or simply dining out, it is likely that you have dreamed of owning your own restaurant. Even non-entrepreneurial types have had the fantasy. I've always loved dining out and fantasized about a unique restaurant where people order ethnic foods in advance that are flown in from all over the world and prepared for special occasions. Obviously this would be quite an undertaking, and a very high-end dining experience. Because it's my fantasy restaurant, I need not worry about the particulars or the costs. If your fantasy involves serving lots of great food to hungry customers but without the high overhead of a restaurant lease, then a food cart, kiosk, trailer, truck, or bustaurant may be for you. These colorful vehicles with their great food, social contact, and audience looking for low-cost eats have made the mobile food industry the latest craze among a new generation of foodies.

The following chapters provide an overview of the mobile food industry and what it takes to start a business here. While the modes of transportation vary, the concept behind the idea of good food and "takin' it to the streets" remains. There is also information about being a business owner. If you embrace this new culture and don't mind the hard work, you could have a marvelous time earning a living as a mobile food entrepreneur.

From Hot Dog Wagons to Bustaurants

Today, a new generation of street food lovers are lining up at food trucks and food carts like never before. Little do they know that neither food trucks nor food carts are new to the streets of American cities. Like so many other popular trends, they are the latest version of a long-standing part of American and world culture. Yet the street food industry has never enjoyed so much publicity or notoriety. It is booming—to the delight of some foodies and the chagrin of others, especially those who own restaurants that are not witnessing the same long lines as their mobile counterparts.

But before taking a look at this burgeoning industry and giving you the lowdown on how to get started, here's a brief lesson in mobile food history. After all, even the modern carmaker knows a little bit about Henry Ford and the growth of the auto industry.

The History of Mobile Food

The concept of mobile food actually began centuries ago when carts brought food to armies at war in Europe and other parts of the world. Farmers also used carts to bring their foods to nearby towns, often stopping to sell goods along the way. In the United States in cities such as New York, immigrants who landed at Ellis Island took jobs selling food from carts. In fact, street food vendors as far back as the 17th century helped New York City's rapid growth, because foods were readily available to merchants, business owners, and inhabitant of the growing city. These foods, however, were mostly taken home to be cooked, rather than eaten straight from the cart. However, not unlike the growing battles between restaurant owners and food truck owners today, public market owners and street food vendors had their share of disputes. In 1691, an ordinance was passed that said food vendors could not open until two hours after the public markets were open.

While carts were around for years, the forerunner of the food truck in the United States was the chuckwagon, which carried food and cooking equipment for the wagon trains as they headed west. In 1866 Charles Goodnight, a Texas rancher, gathered foods in a wagon to accompany long cattle drives. The chuckwagons were especially strong so they could carry a Dutch oven, a cast iron pot with legs, plus a cook's worktable, utensils, and the food, which was known as chuck. Hence the term "chuckwagon." Stew, roast beef, grits, boiled potatoes, beans, and fruit pies were typically on the chuckwagon menus.

Shortly thereafter, in 1872, the first diner was established. It was in a trailer. Diners—complete with service counters dominating the interior, a food preparation area against the back wall, and floor-mounted stools for the customers—were a means of bringing restaurants to new locations in the 1920s and '30s. Many were modeled after railroad dining cars. Some took on the art deco design of the time, and most were pulled on flat back trucks.

The next significant mobile food vehicles were World War I mobile canteens, also known as field kitchens. Often field kitchens were made up of two pieces: the supply section and the rear oven area. These original trailers, typically pulled by horses, evolved into mobile canteen trucks of World War II, providing food and drinks for soldiers as they returned from overseas. When the war ended, the idea of mobile food continued. The proliferation of highways led to the growing suburbs, and as a result, offices and factories also began to spread out, moving away from the big cities. As a result, early snack trucks became common at factories and construction sites.

It was also in the postwar years of the early 1950s that ice cream trucks began cruising the suburbs, to the delight of children in both the United States and Canada. On the early ice cream trucks, the driver would turn a crank to sound the chimes and let it be known that the ice cream truck was on the way. The ice cream was kept cold by blocks of dry ice. Of course by the 1950s, food carts had already become a staple at amusement parks and other venues where people gathered for fun. In fact, it was in 1936 that Oscar Mayer rolled out the first portable hot dog cart and called it the Wiener mobile. It was a big hit.

From the 1960s and '70s on, sandwich trucks and lunch wagons, as they were called, became a staple in all parts of America. Meanwhile, urban areas, tight for space, were able to squeeze in numerous hot dog, ice cream, soda, and pretzel carts wherever foot traffic was heavy. By the late 20th century, there was enough modern technology available to make it more feasible to keep a wider range of foods fresh cooked and served from a mobile vehicle. As a result, today's food truck owner and mobile caterer have more options than ever before.

The Industry Is Booming

There are approximately 3 million food trucks operating in the United States today. A small but growing number are considered gourmet trucks. In addition, there are more than 5 million food carts plus an unknown number of kiosks, which have appeared in malls as well as at train and bus stations, airports, stadiums, conference centers, resorts, and other locations in recent years.

Food industry observers claim that the food truck business is increasing in recent years largely in response to the slow-growing economy. People are seeking inexpensive breakfasts and/or lunches. Also, employees today are often pressed for time, with more work and shorter lunch hours. These factors make the mobile food concept more appealing than ever.

From an entrepreneurial standpoint, kiosks, carts, trailers, and food trucks have a lower overhead than restaurants and can be moved if one location does not generate

Tip...

Smart Tip

While the mobility of a cart, trailer, or truck sounds appealing and even liberating as one drives from place to place, most successful mobile food vehicles find they spend the vast majority of time in a few regular locations.

enough business. Rather than having to determine where to open a restaurant and worry about the old real estate adage "location, location, location," the owner can actually drive to a new location, location, location if business is poor.

The Benefits of Mobile Food

Because food is a necessity and you add the convenience of having food favorites right outside a particular location—or inside with a kiosk—you meet several needs by serving mobile food. First, you offer food that is cost friendly because you need not pay wait people or busboys. You also offer the convenience of quick service. In many cases you provide food choices that can save those on a busy schedule from the need to sit down. Typically they can eat street foods while en route to their next destination. Finally, mobile food is often fun to eat and (if it's good) great to talk about.

The Increase in Mobile Food Businesses

In a slow economy, many people want to try other skills that they were not using at those desk jobs from which they were let go. For others, it's a chance to take on a second way of making money. Then there are restaurant owners who want to make up for falling profits, while also using mobile vehicles to market their brick-and-mortar businesses.

The boom is partly the result of new technology that allows for safer, cost-effective food preparation inside a mobile vehicle. From freezers to ovens to grills, the latest innovations offer more possibilities. Additionally, cleaning products have made it easier to keep a vehicle sanitary and up to code—a long-time concern and major criticism of food trucks.

There are also well-known food companies—from fast food chains like Sprinkles Cupcakes or Johnny Rockets to food manufacturers such as Taste D-Lite or Colorado's organic burrito makers EVOL—who are taking trucks to the streets to increase sales and/or market their brands.

Yes, there are many reasons why the mobile truck industry is going bananas, so to speak. Although there aren't many banana-themed food trucks . . . yet.

FYI

It's important to serve ready-to-eat foods. More than 91 percent of revenue for street vendors comes from the sale of take-away food and drink for immediate consumption rather than for later consumption at another location, according to IBIS World a national publisher of industry research reports.

Can Food Trucks Be Profitable?

While this is not the typical scenario (yet), Joshua Henderson, 36, trained as a chef at the Culinary Institute of America and cooked at the Avalon Hotel in Beverly Hills. He now owns two lunch trucks that drive the streets of Seattle. Each truck serves about 200 lunches every day, and Mr. Henderson says he grossed about $400,000 last year, his first year in business, with only one truck in operation. Courtesy of the *Wall Street Journal* 6/5/09.

Goin' Mobile: Your Options

Even before you decide what foods to sell, you'll want to consider how you want to sell them. We will talk later in greater detail about these mobile possibilities, but for now it's a good idea to familiarize yourself with the most popular options, which include food kiosks, carts, trucks, and busses. Yes, you could probably use a motorcycle or bicycle to your advantage, but we'll leave those to your creative ability.

Clearly, your decision on how to sell your foods will depend on:

- Your startup money, budget, and potential for returns
- Your commitment to the business: part time, full time, etc.
- Your creative ideas and what it will take to fulfill them
- Your experience at running a business
- The size of the business you want to start.
- Your ideal demographic (Obviously if you plan to work inside of local shopping malls, a kiosk is a better plan than a food truck.)

These are a few of the considerations you will look at as you proceed, but for now, let's introduce the common mobile food entities.

Food Kiosks

While the word kiosk is still fairly new to most Westerners, it actually dates back to the 13th century when they were set up in places such as India, Persia, and Pakistan to sell goods.

In modern times, electronic information kiosks have become popular as a means of pushing buttons to gather data. However, food kiosks, not unlike those used seven centuries ago, are essentially booths or food stands that are temporary or mobile facilities used to prepare and sell food. Malls and stadiums are popular locations for food kiosks, which sell anything from pretzels to ice cream to hot dogs to more elaborate fare.

Although kiosks may have wheels, they are not mobile under their own power and in most cases need to be assembled. Most kiosks are rectangular and have room for two people to work within or stand behind, preparing and serving the food. They also have counter space and overhead signage.

The low overhead, flexibility, and ease by which a kiosk can be opened and closed are among the reasons why they're so popular. They are also an excellent choice in areas where your outdoor selling season would be limited by cold or nasty weather. Of course, the size of the kiosk limits the inventory, so it's important for a kiosk owner to carry as much as possible and price accordingly so that she can make money off of what is on hand each day. Because they are usually operating indoors, kiosk owners typically sign licensing agreements at malls, stadiums, movie theaters, or other locations. Many major food businesses such as Ben & Jerry's and Baskin-Robbins franchise express kiosks.

Food Carts and Concession Trailers

The food cart and the concession trailer have been around for decades and combined are a multibillion-dollar industry today. The best known have always been hot dog and ice cream carts. They are among the most cost-effective ways to start a mobile food business because the carts are typically pulled by your car, truck, van, or pushed by hand. Food is either prepared in advance, purchased ready to sell—like ice cream pops or cups of Italian ices—then stored, and either heated up or pulled from the freezer. Carts are also fairly easy to maintain and in many counties and communities require less licensing than the full-sized food trucks. It is also cost effective if you choose to own several carts and hire friends, family, or outside employees to help run them for you.

Unlike kiosks, which are typically found indoors (although they can be outdoors), food carts are typically outdoor businesses. An advantage of a food cart is easy mobility. Because food carts do not take up much room, it is easy to change locations.

There are two basic types of food carts. One has room for the vendor to sit or stand inside and serve food through a window. The other utilizes all the space in the cart for food storage and cooking equipment, which is typically a grill. The precise type of cart is determined largely by the food being offered. Espresso and coffee carts, for example, are made specifically with hot beverages in mind.

Modern day food cart owners have cleaned up the somewhat greasy reputation of street food vendors. They have also expanded their menus. Kebobs and gyros came on the cart scene awhile ago, and vegetarian and Mediterranean salads have also caught on, as well as fish and chips. The Euro Trash food cart in Portland, Oregon, for example, offers items like a prawn baguette with Portuguese curry prawns. And then there's the Pie Lab, with slices of pie for $4, plus $1 for ice cream or whipped cream.

Trailers, like carts, do not move under their own power, limiting their potential locations. Food trailers are often found at fairs, carnivals, sporting events, or other places where they can be unhitched and sit for awhile. Unlike most carts, trailers allow for cooking and have room for two or three people inside. Skillet Street Food in Seattle operates from an Airstream trailer with a full kitchen within. In short, a trailer can provide more options than a cart but is still less expensive than a truck.

Food Trucks

The food truck can carry any number of foods, and in some cases more sophisticated equipment for storing, serving, cooking, and preparing foods. The traditional food trucks were known for providing lunches, typically stocking sandwiches, kebobs, tacos, burgers, and other standard fare for the lunch crowd. Many have expanded to include healthier vegetarian and vegan offerings, as well as the not-so-healthy barbeque ribs. They do big business in corporate parks and places that have limited access to restaurants. Most food trucks are stocked from concessionaires, but there is a growing number that are associated with fast food and mid-level restaurants. Sizzler and California Pizza Kitchen, for example, are putting together their own food trucks as are other chains.

Larger than carts, trucks can carry more food and handle more business. However, food trucks need more space to park both when doing business and when "off-duty."

Essentially, there are two types of food trucks. One is the mobile food preparation vehicle (MFPV) where food is prepared as customers wait, hopefully not very long. The other is the industrial catering vehicle (ICV), which sells only prepackaged foods. An MFPV costs more than an ICV, and both cost more than a food cart. For example, a used hotdog cart may cost under $2,500, while a retro-fitted used food truck would typically cost $30,000 or more. A newly designed food truck retrofitted MFPV with new all equipment could cost you upwards of $100,000.

Complying with additional health department rules and regulations can also drive up food truck costs. Clearly, a smaller truck, a used truck, and/or a truck with

Smart Tip

It is recommended that you start with a few items that you know how to prepare well and expand as you grow. Carts and kiosks typically sell a couple of items. Food truck owners should follow suit. It makes starting and running your business much easier.

limited equipment costs less. Therefore, it is up to you to determine whether you'll be cooking in the truck, preparing food off-site and serving from the vehicle, or selling prepared and prepackaged foods.

Gourmet Food Trucks

Basically the same as a food truck, the gourmet food truck takes food quality to a higher level. Of the 4,000 food trucks licensed to do business in the Los Angeles area, only about 115 are considered "gourmet." They are run by ambitious young chefs who offer cuisine not typically found in food trucks, such as specialty crepes, Kimchi pork-fries, osso bouco, velvet cupcakes, or the chicken marsala meatballs with cilantro chutney found in the Great Balls on Tires gourmet food truck. Like Great Balls on Tires, many gourmet trucks have specialties and themes. In addition, they let their clientele know where they'll be parked through their websites and social media sites like Twitter. While food trucks need not have kitchens, gourmet trucks are more likely to have food prepared on the spot—and high-end food at that.

At the start of the new gourmet food truck craze, Los Angeles was clearly the place to find such high-end dining. Now, however, New York had gained its share of such fancy food vehicles, such as the Rickshaw Dumpling Bar and The Dessert Truck,

The Border Grill Truck serves up gourmet tacos, quesadillas, ceviches, and other Mexican favorites in and around the Los Angeles area.

founded by a former Le Cirque pastry chef. And as the concept of serving fine food rolls along, other cities from Portland, Oregon, to St Louis and on down to Miami's South Beach are jumping on the foodie bandwagon with their own regional favorites. Food Network chef Ingrid Hoffmann's black and pink Latin Burger and Taco Truck, for example, has become quite the rage in Miami.

Major Market Segments

Street locations/corners	55.0%
Other locations/venues/events	18.0%
Industrial/construction work sites	15.0%
Shopping malls	12.0%

(Statistics from IBISWorld)

The Mobile Catering Business

Mobile catering trucks can be defined in a variety of ways and can overlap with mobile food trucks. For my purposes here, I'll highlight three differences. First, a catering truck is hired for a specific event such as a picnic, party, or fair. Secondly, the person hiring the catering vehicle can select from a catering menu. Third, a catering vehicle can be used to transport the foods, which are then handed out from inside the truck or set up at the event or gathering, typically on trays or buffet style.

This can mean providing the food to be served outdoors or parking and serving from the truck as the food trucks do. The differences are primarily in the manner of doing business. Nonetheless, the need for a reliable vehicle, licensing, permits, sanitary conditions, a business plan, and startup money are quite similar to the requirements of a mobile food business.

One of the advantages of a mobile catering business is that you are not risking as much in inventory because you are cooking and bringing food as ordered for the party. Therefore, you are covered for your food costs. You also have a specific destination, so you need not worry whether or not your favorite destinations will be busy or not. Typically, you are less dependent on good weather because many catered functions will be indoors. As long as you can get there with the food, you are usually OK. Of course, you do need to line

> **FYI**
>
> Have you heard of the 80–20 rule in sales? This is a long-standing business principle that says that 80 percent of your business will come from repeat customers and 20 percent from new customers. For caterers or mobile food vendors, this means, as the Simon and Garfunkel song says, "Keep the Customer Satisfied."

up enough work to support your business. The difference between a mobile catering business and other catering businesses is that you are using the mobility of the truck to show up rather than having a catering hall or venue.

The mobile catering business affords you flexibility as to when you take jobs and where. Still, the more available you are, the better off you will be.

Bustaurants

As the name implies, a bustaurant is not a truck but a bus, often a double-decker with the lower level for the kitchen and the upper level for customers to sit and eat. They are new. Some boast gourmet foods, while others have more standard fare. The idea is to provide seating and be a restaurant on wheels. Mostly found in the San Francisco and Los Angeles areas thus far, they may be the trend of the future. Needless to say, they require more room to park and additional licensing in most counties, and are more costly to start because the buses need to be fully refurbished to include grills, refrigerators, vents, and so on. Many food trucks, on the other hand, are designed and built with both cooking and serving food in mind.

Some bustaurants, such as Diamond Lil, a converted 1957 Greyhound bus, take diners on a private mobile eating adventure. Others park and serve customers as they board at a specific location. Some of the buses cook the food while parked— it's illegal to cook while the bus is in motion, at least in California—while others bring prepared food cooked prior to parking. Because they are very new, more and more innovative bustaurants will literally be rolling out as you read this book. Yet because they are so new, the jury is still out on whether they are a passing fad (pun intended) or they will catch on. Much of what is discussed here as necessary for food trucks is also necessary for bustaurants, including marketing, costs, permits, menus, etc.

Your Customers

According to the Small Business Development Center National Information Clearinghouse (SBDCNET), as of 2008 young adults and parents with children at home were the leading buyers of mobile foods. You'll also find that the most money was spent by 25- to 34-year-olds who averaged $44 a month in expenditures and were closely followed by 34- to 44-year-olds, at $41 per month.

There are several demographic groups that can provide potential customers. Who you focus on influences your menu, locations, and daily schedule of food preparation.

The Breakfast Club

First you want to be ready for the morning crowd. Coffee is your number-one priority, so make sure you are making it fresh and good. Your customers want a good cup of coffee on their way to work, with maybe a Danish, bagel, or croissant. You'll get some juice lovers, so be prepared. Fruit is also a new, healthy, morning favorite. If you're parked by office parks or on streets lined with office buildings, expect a lot of people on their way into the office. This breakfast club does not usually stop for an elaborate breakfast, so keep it simple. Be ready with easy-to-serve foods, and give them their shot of caffeine with a friendly smile to start their day. More than any other group, these customers operate from force of habit. If they like your food, coffee, prices, and quickness, they'll come back again and again without even thinking about it.

The Lunch Bunch

This is the bread-and-butter group for many truck and cart owners, no pun intended (well, maybe). Here you can be more diverse in your offerings because the lunch crowd has more time to decide what they want than the breakfast club, whose members are often on the run.

However, whether you are parked by a construction site or the corporate offices of a Fortune 500 company, there is still a time element to contend with. You need to be able to serve and move on to the next customer quickly. Typically, if someone has 45 minutes to an hour for lunch (and in today's overworked corporate culture, many people have just 15 minutes to grab the food to eat at their desks), you want to minimize the lines by being ready to take orders and serve. After all, if customers have time to wait around, they can sit in a restaurant.

Your other advantage is prices below those in restaurants, so keep them down. Zach Brooks of midtownlunch.com says $10 is the typical cutoff point for most street foods.

Much of today's lunch bunch is also looking for creative and healthy choices, although many will still go with the standard hot dog or taco and soda. If you can, mix it up a little between standard fare and your creative ideas. Lunchers usually travel in pairs (or more), and they may not all have the sophisticated tastes. Ethnic cuisine is a favorite, but again, consider milder and more mainstream options for a wider lunch crowd. Keep the menu manageable because the more you offer, the more you need to have in stock—and space is limited.

Tastes for Tourists and Attendees

Tourists, business travelers, and attendees at conferences and special events are around for a reason. Know your customers. The crowd at a NASCAR event probably has different tastes than the attendees at an environmental convention. Stock up accordingly. Tourists are often anxious to taste something that epitomizes your city. If you're at a tourist location, such as Central Park in Manhattan or Coney Island, a New York City hot dog would be a tourist-style treat, as would jambalaya on Bourbon Street in New Orleans.

If you are centered around a theme, such as cupcakes, you'll need to plan your locations accordingly. Of course, products like cupcakes have a wide appeal, so unless other dessert trucks are in an area, you can always find your way into the mix.

The Late Nighters

When the clubs or nighttime sporting events let out, people are hungry. Knowing where to find the late night crowd means knowing the nightlife in your city and being prepared to satisfy their appetites for food or munchies, as the case may be. Typically this crowd is looking for simple snacks. Those who are inebriated and cannot pronounce elaborate dishes, don't usually want them at 2 A.M. Coffee is always a mainstay as are snack foods and hand-held favorites like pizza and tacos.

No Training Necessary

Cody Fields was a mechanical engineer building water treatment plants in South America. He spent five years working, traveling, and eating a lot of empanadas. Finally, the Texas native returned home, settled in Austin, and went back to school. He wanted to do something different but didn't know quite what that new career was going to be. While in school, he met Kristen, who would eventually become his wife. Both Cody and Kristin enjoyed cooking, but neither had any formal training. Cody took a job in a bank and knew it wasn't for him. "The first day at the bank I was seated in a cubical. I immediately knew from day one that I needed to get out of there," says Cody. So, one night in 2007, while attending the opening of a new neighborhood bar, Cody and Kristen cooked six-dozen gourmet empanadas as a grand opening gift to welcome the new bar owners. "They loved the empanadas," recalls Cody, and the bar owner immediately asked how they could get more. "Give me two weeks and I'll get back to you," replied an ambitious Cody. In those two weeks, he rented a commercial kitchen, got his food-manufacturing license, and secured all the necessary permits to start cooking.

Together Cody and Kristen brainstormed ideas for recipes and fillings and after two weeks they were ready to start selling empanadas. Over the next three months the cooking couple picked up a few more clients. The food truck craze had yet to begin in Austin. "There was a cupcake truck and a crepe truck, plus some of the old taco trucks that went to construction sites," he explains.

Cody bought an old pizza truck on eBay for about $20,000 and a generator for another $10,000. He fixed up the truck and got the necessary licenses. He also painted the truck bright red. The truck stood out, and Mmmpanadas was officially on the road. Over the years the Austin Mmmpanadas truck has been written up in *GQ* and twice in *Southern Living*. Cody has long since left that bank job, and the empanadas that he and Kristin continue to make are now sold not only from the truck but also in stores all over Austin, including Whole Foods. They are still looking to expand their retail business. And it all started by cooking 72 gourmet empanadas (mmmpanadas.com).

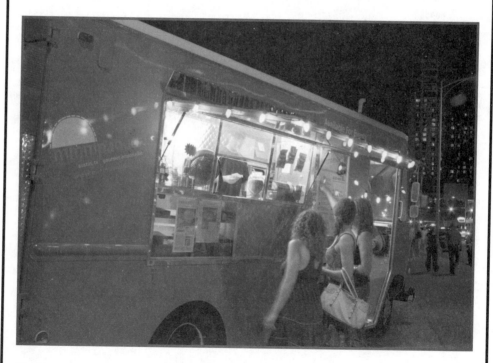

The bright red Mmmpanadas truck services the night crowd in Austin, Texas.

Planning a Business

As exciting as it may seem to jump into a new business, it doesn't happen without significant planning, at least if you want to have a good chance of success. To start, you need to have the right mind-set and the skills to go into the business of your dreams. You also need to understand what it takes to be an entrepreneur. It usually starts with a great idea or an opportunity that presents itself, such as buying into an existing business or a franchise.

In this chapter we take a look at the first part of the business equation—you, the business owner. Then we look at some of the planning that you will want to do before venturing out into the field, or in this case, hitting the streets.

Are You Hungry?

Starting a business means being your own boss. It also means getting ready to roll up your sleeves and get greasy if necessary. The mobile food business is going strong. You'll want to act fast, before too many players get into the game. There is only so much room on the streets. In fact, many city governments are aware that a limit on licenses may be necessary, if it's not already on the books (such as in New York City). Nonetheless, you cannot take too many shortcuts. Learning about the business inside and out is key to starting any venture.

To earn money in mobile food service means being hungry. It means having menu items your competitors don't have (or at least making your own unique versions of popular favorites) and finding locations that aren't already teeming with competitors.

Mobile lunch trucks have long been based upon the simple concept of bringing quality food to people in areas where there are not many other food choices. Now it is also about bringing cost-friendly options to places where there are other food choices. Faster service and lower prices allow you to compete with brick-and-mortar eateries. However, to succeed you need to serve good food and maintain the highest levels of cleanliness.

To do these things well, you need not only a can-do attitude but also an eye for detail because there are numerous details involved. You also need to be organized, able to set up and follow a working routine, and be ready to make changes if your routine isn't working. You don't need to be a chef, but knowing how to cook is a big plus. You can, however, simply know quality food, and/or have great marketing abilities. And finally you also need a little bit of daring

Beware!
While food carts and trucks are competitive among themselves, they do share one commonality. Neither is particularly well liked by many brick-and-mortar business owners, especially restaurateurs and food shop owners. Reports of such business owners calling the cops on food trucks abound. Other incidents from slashed tires to harassed customers have also been reported. Because you are the newcomer, you need to be aware and respectful of business owners and do your best to avoid ruffling their feathers.

because running a food truck isn't a standard office job or restaurant position. It means running a mobile enterprise where you may be in several locations each week, some for better and some for worse.

Do You Have the Drive?

While it may look easy, the food truck industry takes a lot of hard work. For Scott Baitinger and partner Steve Mai who run the famous Streetza pizza truck in Milwaukee, Wisconsin, a typical day starts three or four hours before taking the truck out on the road. "First we'll stop at Sam's Club or Restaurant Depot and pick up fresh ingredients. Then we go to our off-site commissary kitchen where we do all the prep work, which includes rolling the dough, making sauces, cutting the vegetables, and all of the things you really can't do in a 10-by-10 truck," explains Baitinger, who still works a day job in advertising but handles the truck on nights and weekends. Mai runs the weekday shifts except at times in the winter when nobody in Milwaukee wants to trek outside in three feet of snow—not even for pizza.

Then the Streetza team, which also includes a small staff on various shifts, park at well-selected locations and prepare and sell foods. "We put on the toppings and assemble and bake the food in the truck, but because of the size of pizzas, it's not the kind of thing you can make on the truck." Some vendors sell food that can be cooked on their trucks, notes Baitinger. Some cities allow cooking on a vehicle, while others require a separate, off-site commercial kitchen be used. This requirement differs from city to city.

At the end of a day, which is typically when they run out of food or the crowds have dissipated, comes the cleanup. "It's a lot like a restaurant cleanup with stainless steel cleaners, scrubbing, mopping, and making sure everything is in perfect shape to start again tomorrow," adds Baitinger.

Most mobile food business owners follow a similar set routine, whether it includes running the kiosk, cart, or truck themselves or having employees run it. The routine, as is the case with Streetza, may include very early morning food shopping a few days a week, if not everyday. Then there is stocking the kiosk or vehicle and heading to your destination(s). There is also a need to take some time during the day for marketing,

Smart Tip

By hand or on your computer, map out your day. Having your schedule on paper allows you to look closely and possibly find ways to improve it. A printed version also lets you hire employees and plug them into the routine more easily. Most importantly, your daily or weekly schedule helps you not forget to do something.

and when. Learning how to tweet and use the other popular social media tools is very important for marketing and building up your brand in this new street food culture. In many cases, mobile communication builds a loyal following. Streetza is among the many food trucks that interact regularly with its loyal following via Twitter. This helps it find great locations and receive suggestions for menu items. The fans even named the Streetza truck. Today, Twitter helps food trucks draw a crowd much like the jingle of the Mr. Softee truck brought kids running for ice cream.

Stamina

It may not be a skill, but being in shape helps in the mobile food business. Consider the lifting, standing, and movement involved in a typical day. Adria Shimada who owns the Parfait Ice Cream truck in Seattle noted that when she started out in the business she didn't realize how exhausting it could be. "You've got to be in fairly good shape," says Adria, who, with help, works on loading the truck, moving vats of ice cream in and out of freezers, serving from the truck, and standing in her commissary making fresh homemade organic (and wonderful) ice cream for hours.

Number Skills

You need not be a math major, but having a good head for number is a big plus. From recipes and measurements in the kitchen to bookkeeping, pricing, calculating profit margins, and keeping an eye on your budget, you will use plenty of numbers every day. Your calculator can help, but you need to be able to make determinations about whether the numbers it gives you look good or not.

Can You Compete?

Because the mobile food business is growing quickly, you need to have a competitive nature to succeed, especially in Los Angeles where food trucks are lining the streets. You need a keen eye for finding a competitive edge, that special something that sets you apart from the other trucks, trailers, busses, carts, or kiosks. The same goes for mobile catering businesses.

While competition is discussed in greater detail in the marketing section, it is important that you go into business with the idea that you are not just another fish in a giant pond, or you will get swallowed up. To be competitive:

- You need to approach the business with an eye for what your competitors are doing.
- You need to see which food trucks are generating the longest lines and why.

- You need to know your competitors' prices.
- You need to find out which mobile catering company is at the top of people's lists and figure out what it offers.
- You need to approach business with the keen eye of a detective, looking for clues that tell you why one company is succeeding and another is not.

Part of your prebusiness acumen should be due diligence. If you don't do your homework, you will likely fail in a competitive business. Market research is one of the first steps in starting any business. Scoping out the competition in this case is imperative because the competition may be five miles away one day and parked right across the street the next.

> **Tip...**
>
> **Smart Tip**
>
> Get into social media, and read what the foodies are saying about their favorite mobile food vendors and local restaurants. Get a feel for their favorite ideas from food to promotional items. Find out what the culture is all about, and show up at some of the food truck locations. Besides tasting the food of your competitors, you'll want to get a feel for the buzz. Talk to customers, and when you're on your own jot down notes on what you have learned.

Business Goals

Mobile food success falls into several categories depending largely on what the owners are seeking from the business. Your goals will be based on your own situation, including your lifestyle, desired income, and other business endeavors.

Starting a business means you have the opportunity to take a new direction, or even many directions since you are mobile. Running a business provides an opportunity to follow your own dreams. It allows you to express yourself as well as make a living on your own schedule. Yes, you will need persistence and hard work to make a go of a new business. Yes, there will be times you question whether or not it will be worth it. And yes, there will be times when you may need to shift gears and make some major changes. A positive aspect is that as a business owner you are in control and everything comes back to you. Of course the negative aspect is that as a business owner you are in control and everything comes back to you. Clearly, there are two sides to taking on such responsibility. You get the glory and to enjoy the profits when all goes well. You get blame and have to deal with the losses when all goes poorly.

So, why start a business?

- To be in charge
- To have greater flexibility

- For personal expression
- To utilize specific skills (often those not used when working for someone else)
- To better control your own destiny
- To have an opportunity to do better financially
- To be socially and environmentally responsible
- To interact with your community
- To create jobs for other people
- To work with family, friends, and people you actually like

These are among the reasons to start any new business. Hopefully some are among your reasons for starting a mobile food business.

Part-Time Business

For some people, running a mobile food business on the weekends and/or at night can provide an extra source of income. However, as Cody Fields of Mmmpanadas found out after a year of having a desk job by day and driving the food truck by night, it can become quite exhausting. In addition, the cost of buying and maintaining a full-sized truck may not be offset by part-time usage. Scott Baitinger has kept his full-time day job in marketing by having a partner and staff running the truck on a full-time schedule. It all depends on your situation. Some owners have enough money to hire people to run the truck while others use business partners, taking a behind-the-scenes role.

Some kiosk owners and food cart owners find that working weekends at special events can supplement a full-time income. It's still a lot of work, but overhead is lower than with a truck and there are profits to be made if the location is good.

Weekend mobile caterers have found that running their business on the side can be productive only if they take on what they can handle and have an inexpensive vehicle for transport. Remember, the more money you put into the vehicle, the more you need to recoup. If you keep expenses low, you can make money on a part-time basis with good marketing, a good product, and a schedule that is manageable. But don't book more than you can handle.

Full-Time Business

Full time means making the "big" commitment. You need enough volume to make this work and that comes from:

- Scouting the competition
- Learning the business
- Making sure you adhere to every city, town, and local ordinance
- Having all necessary permits and licenses and updating them regularly
- Having a good product that you've tested again and again
- Knowing your territory well
- Knowing your demographics
- Budgeting time and money wisely
- Setting up a daily and weekly routine and re-working it until it runs like clockwork
- Marketing, marketing, and marketing some more
- Rolling up your sleeves and working hard
- Hiring people you can count on and training them well
- Remembering to do your bookkeeping

Smart Tip

Tip...

Set a weekly time on your calendar to handle book-keeping, paying taxes, paying bills, etc. It's very easy in your busy schedule to forget about these simple, yet vital, business requirements. Select a time and a place and enter it on your calendar, Blackberry, computer scheduling program, or any place else that helps you remember to take care of these business needs regularly.

Like most brick-and-mortar retail businesses, you need to have enough sales with a sufficient profit margin to make this endeavor worthwhile. Your advantages are that you will have a lower overhead than most brick-and-mortar businesses and you can change locations far more easily. Your disadvantages are that you can only charge so much for street food and your hours of operation are limited by various factors, including parking restrictions, the weather, and your inventory.

Extension of a Current Business

If you own a restaurant or if you are a food manufacturer, you may now be joining the many entrepreneurs taking their businesses to the streets. Even McDonald's is now readying trucks. For many existing restaurant owners or food manufacturers like Cody Fields, the outside of the truck is "a giant (28-foot) billboard." It helps advertise his wholesale empanadas business. The idea of getting the brand name out there is a tremendous plus when it comes to customer awareness. It is also a tasty way of getting your product in the mouths of more people.

EVOL, the Boulder, Colorado-based makers of all-natural frozen burritos, is also extending its lucrative wholesale business to food trucks. "The plan is to get our brand

and product into the hands of people in cool places, like ski resorts, stadiums, surf contests, and at the Bolder Boulder, which is the biggest 10k in country," says Phil Anson, EVOL founder and CEO. However, EVOL will be doing something quite different than most food trucks by giving away mini-burritos at these large events. "Our goal, or marketing strategy, is to get our product into as many people's mouths as we can to create authentic honest conversions at the grocery stores," he explains. "People at a ski resort or an event will be exposed to the food, the packaging, and the branding," adds Anson, who estimates that the company may give away as many as 300,000 to 400,000 mini-burritos in 2011. Not unlike samples of products handed out in grocery stores, the concept is to use a food truck as a means of advertising and marketing for the business, rather than paying a fortune on commercials where buyers cannot taste the product.

Restaurant owners in other cities are using similar plans to sell or give out samples to draw customers to their establishments. The mobility allows them to reach different demographic audiences and, as Anson is doing, get their foods and their brand to places where the people are.

The Business Plan

Regardless of your entrepreneurial vision, a business plan is important in any endeavor, especially if you are hoping to attract some backers to help you foot the bill for that $75,000 specially refurbished truck you have your eye on. A well thought out business plan tells the story of your entrepreneurial dream and details your vision in a way that it can help you generate the necessary funding.

Even if you are not seeking backers, a business plan can help guide you through the process of gathering all the key information to keep you on track as you proceed.

There are books, articles, websites, and software packages designed to take you through the steps necessary to build a business plan. They usually come complete with templates to follow so you need not recreate the wheel. The inclusion of some business plan basics here is designed to get you to start thinking about possibilities, which you can fill in as you read through this book and decide on what kind of food(s) you'll be serving, the size of your vehicle, and your startup and operational costs.

A business plan is a way of organizing on paper all of the pieces of the puzzle, from your equipment needs to your various locations to ordering and shopping for food. Finally, it is a living, breathing document that can not only serve as a benchmark and also can be altered and expanded as your business grows and changes over the years.

Included in a typical business plan are the following:

1. *Executive summary.* This is a short, broad yet enticing summary of the business. What is the business all about, and why are you excited about it? Although it usually appears first, this section is often written last, after you have put all the pieces in place.

2. *Products and/or services.* Here you can include specific items that you will sell or services you will offer. Include foods and/or drinks that will be on your menu and other possibilities that you anticipate adding down the road. Explain their popularity and why they will be sought by your customers. Also explain what goes into making these culinary delights.

3. *Industry analysis.* Here you paint a picture of the mobile food industry in which your business will be a player. From your research, talk about the big picture and the growing popularity of mobile foods and catering. Back up your statements with facts and numbers. By researching and writing a few paragraphs on the mobile food business, you will also learn more about the industry.

4. *Competitive analysis.* This is huge! Do your research carefully and know whom you are up against. Be realistic. Listing the strengths and weaknesses of your direct competitors helps you determine where you will fit into the local market. Then see if you can provide something that your competitors do not offer. Do you have more menu options? Perhaps you have a combo with a drink that is cheaper than your competitor's prices. Maybe you've even created a new food combination like the Pirito, a flat rectangular cross between a panini and a burrito (golden crispy pita bread on outside and any number of foods inside) created by Josh Lanahan and Michelle Lozuaway for the Fresh Local truck in Portsmouth, New Hampshire. Know your competition well and seek a competitive edge.

5. *Marketing and sales.* Once you have the details in place, you need to explain how you will let the world know you are in business. In this section, you discuss your plans for marketing and promoting your mobile food business as well as your plans for selling your products and services. Will you be setting up a website? Do you plan to use social media, such as in Twitter, Facebook, and FourSquare to get the word out about your business and your location?

Where will you be selling? Street locations? Festival and events? Do you do mobile theme catering? Parties? Outdoor events? Office parties?

This is where to define your plan of attack. If you are seeking funding, this section is extremely important because backers want to know that you have thought about what you will be selling, to whom, and how you will reach your audience and build a following. Also include your pricing in conjunction with competitive pricing in your area.

6. *Management.* Another important section is management. Here you let readers know who is running the business. Potential financial backers are particularly interested in this information because they want to know to whom they are lending their money. Include all of the key people involved in making your business happen. If this is a solo venture, use a bio that features applicable experiences in your career or personal life that apply to this venture. It is very important that backers believe in you, so don't sell yourself short.

7. *Operations.* Are you cooking off-truck and bringing the food onboard to be heated? Are you cooking on-truck? As a mobile caterer, will you bring burners and other equipment that must be moved to each location? If you have a trailer or cart, where will you be set up and how often will you change locations? Do you shop for your ingredients? When? Where?

   Carefully think through this section. Much of it depends on what foods you sell, the size of your mobile vehicle, and whether or not you have (or are required to have) an off-site commissary kitchen. Walk yourself through the entire operation step by step to see if it works smoothly. Then write it down.

8. *Financial.* The goal here, with help from your accountant, is to make realistic projections based on researching similar businesses. Here you show the numbers and see where you will make profits—or not. This is a must-do section whether or not you seek a backer. You need to know your profit potential and how long it will take to start showing a profit after purchasing the vehicle and equipment. Also include a cash and balance sheet for a year to show a cash flow. Hint: Be conservative in your financial estimates.

9. *Financial requirements.* If you are seeking funding, include the amount of financing needed, based on the previous sections, to reach your goals. Detail how you will be spending the money you receive from investors. Again, be realistic, research costs carefully, and indicate how much money you anticipate putting into the business venture yourself. Hint: You stand a much greater chance of getting investors interested or bank loan approval if you have invested your own money into the business.

> **Tip...**
>
> **Smart Tip**
> Review your business plan first to make sure it tells the story of the business you envision. Next make sure it covers all of the key areas and leaves no stone unturned when it comes to running your business in a smooth manner. Finally, if you are planning to show your business plan to prospective backers, make sure to proofread it very carefully.

Add any supporting documentation, which may include various financial reports, culinary awards, diplomas, or anything else that highlights your story and a business plan. You also want to make sure to have copies of the licenses necessary to run your mobile food vehicle. Do not try to dazzle prospective readers with hype; provide the real story of the business so that it is clear on paper how it will operate and when you anticipate making money.

Of course, this is a very basic business plan outline. Before you sit down to start writing, you need to do research and look at other business plans in books or online. Websites such as Bplans.com or a computer program such as Biz Plan Pro from Palo Alto software (paloalto.com) can be very helpful.

3

What's On the Menu?

If you look at the food trucks, trailers, carts, and kiosks on the streets and at mobile catering menus, you'll find that almost anything edible can be served up street side. Of course the big question is: How practical is it? This may account for the lack of baked Alaska carts out there, but rest assured, someone is probably selling it on some street corner.

Planning Your Mobile Menu

Determining what to serve can be fun. But there are a lot of factors to consider when it comes to menu planning in the mobile food world. Here are a few:

- What do you know how to cook?
- What foods do you enjoy cooking?
- What foods are popular in your town, county, city, or region?
- What ingredients are easy to get from wholesalers, markets, or farms in your area?
- What foods are easy to transport to and from an off-site commercial kitchen?
- What can you prepare and/or heat up without much difficulty?
- What food(s) are ideally suited for your culinary expertise or allow you to try creative new recipes?
- What foods can customers easily carry around with them?
- What food(s) are potentially cost effective for you to sell?
- What foods are not being sold at 100 other food trucks, carts, kiosks, or mobile caterers in your area?
- What times of day will you be open for business? Breakfast? Lunch? Dinner? Late night? All of the above?
- Are you going to specialize in one or two foods with several variations such as pizza, tacos, or ice cream? Are you going to have a larger menu?

> **FYI**
>
> As of 2010, there is a steadily increasing demand for cheap, freshly prepared food among 18- to 44-year-olds, according to the National Restaurant Association.

Remember, a larger menu typically requires more space and may move you from a kiosk or cart to a truck or bus.

The Next Step

Unless you are buying prepared foods or have a chef providing you with foods, you'll want to plan your own recipes, work on them, re-work them, and have some taste tests. Consider your family and friends as your very own guinea pigs. Have parties, make a fun time of it, but get them to taste your foods and give you honest critiques. Don't be afraid of some criticism—better to receive it from friends and family than from food critics and customers.

Beware!

Don't start out with foods you have not thoroughly tested. This means you need to perfect each recipe to be sure it has the following qualities:

1. It is easy to make repeatedly in large quantities.
2. It tastes consistently good.
3. It is easy to serve.
4. It travels well.

Once you've found a few favorites, make sure you can master the recipes. Write them down for future reference. Next, try some variations on a theme. Most mobile food entrepreneurs spend several months, often while waiting for their truck to be retrofitted and their backers to fork over some startup money, experimenting with various menu items.

Another important consideration is the culture of the town in which you will be serving your foods. You may want to gear your menu to a younger audience in a college town or to a specific ethnic culture in a neighborhood made up of immigrants. In big cities, you may be able to select the neighborhoods that suit your style. You'll find neighborhoods where the gourmet foodies hang out as well as places where there are sports fans or the nightclubbers. Some areas are just right for tacos, and other areas have plenty of kids (and adults) looking for ice cream and cupcakes.

Menu Ideas

Now it's time to put on your thinking cap or chef's hat as the case may be. Below are some of the basics that foodies are finding at their favorite mobile food services. No, we don't want you to steal these culinary goodies, simply get some ideas for your own unique slant on popular menu items.

The Basics

- Sandwiches
- Wraps
- Salads
- Hot dogs
- Hamburgers
- Pizza
- Tacos

Tip...

Smart Tip

Know the zoning ordinances in your area. If, for example, you want to sell ice cream but cannot park anywhere near local schools or playgrounds. You can only park in certain downtown business areas, where maybe ice cream won't be as popular as lunch foods. See if your planned food ideas can be sold in areas where your customers are found.

- Tortillas
- Gyros

It's hard to go wrong with basic food truck and food cart staples, especially if you put your own spin on them. The possibilities for sandwiches, hot dogs, burgers, pizza toppings, and salads are mind-boggling. How about a nicoise sandwich like that of New York's Tangiers Bocadillo, packed with tuna, hard-boiled egg, veggies, and French fries—yes, fries in the sandwich! You could think along the same lines as the MIHO Gastrotruck in San Diego, where you can find a famous Stuffed Pork Loin Sandwich with all natural Duroc pork loin stuffed with bacon, local wild mushrooms, local braised greens, and walnuts, cranberry orange relish, Dijon aioli, gouda, and local rosemary focaccia.

If you prefer the more standard dog cart or burger wagon, why not opt for a hot dog with some flare like the We Be Weiners Chili Dog in Portland, Oregon, with chili, chopped onions, and grated jack cheese, topped with yellow mustard, ketchup, and relish. Or think along the lines of Seattle Skillet Street food with a burger of grass fed beef, plus arugula, bacon jam, and cambozola served on a soft roll.

If you want to stand out from your competitors, you'll want to try various slants on flavorful favorites. You can mix it up a little, but always serve some basic basics for the less adventurous crowd. Scout your competition, know your demographics, and get a feel for how innovative you can get. And remember, there's nothing wrong with a standard hot dog cart. They have been a staple on the street corners of New York City for generations. In fact, the Coney Island hot dog carts are still legendary. It works if your food tastes good!

One of the best things about going with the basics is that they are usually easy to purchase in quantity and easy to find. Food like hot dogs, gyros, and tacos are easy on-the-go foods that are especially popular with those looking to grab a quick lunch while being mobile themselves. Also consider buying from organic food vendors.

And don't forget breakfast. You can go with the more standard eggs on a roll, English muffins, blueberry muffins, and waffles, or be creative like Los Angeles's Buttermilk Truck with its red velvet chocolate chip pancakes or Portsmouth's Fresh Local truck with its vanilla custard French toast.

Smart Tip

Tip...

Shop around for the paper goods you will need and find plenty of storage space. Because they are not perishable, load up in quantity to get the good bulk rate on things like napkins, straws, and coffee stirrers. If you buy enough from a nearby warehouse, you should be able to have them delivered.

Gourmet Delights

- Lamb and beef specialties

- Designer potatoes
- Duck delights
- Designer crepes
- Escargot
- Crème brûleé
- Maine lobster rolls
- Shrimp sandwiches

One of the primarily reasons for the latest mobile food craze is that some of today's vehicles are serving up restaurant quality fine foods. While these eclectic dishes may not suit everyone's preference for a simple lunch, they do offer some upscale culinary delights at reasonable prices. In some cases, the trucks actually provide mobile tasting menus for established fine dining restaurants.

The keys to a gourmet food truck are having a gourmet chef and a means of transporting more temperamental flavors without stirring up trouble. A well-known chef can make a difference because she likely has a following. Jody Maroni's Sausage Kingdom was the first Kitchen Kingdom to serve gourmet sausages, including the Yucatan sausage with cilantro and chicken apple sausage. Jody was well known in the Southern California area long before gourmet food trucks hit the streets. So, when her truck emerged, she had an instant following. Likewise, when well-known chef Biagio Barone (who owns Biagio's Osteria, Zagats' top-rated Italian Restaurant in Connecticut), decided to open his gourmet food truck, GotChef, in Milford, Connecticut, people took notice. Got Chef serves dishes like Sirloin Pinwheels (aka steak rolled with gorgonzola cheese and wild mushrooms) as well as Osso Bucco Milanese.

As for taking foods on the road, sure, hot dogs, tacos and gyros travel well, while foods like flank steak marinated in lime, garlic, cilantro, and beer from Roy Choi's Match Truck may require a little more planning. But rest assured that nearly anything you or your gourmet chef can cook can be transported with enough due diligence on your part. The tricks are to find the right equipment and make sure you have the proper temperature to keep your foods at their best.

One of the keys to the success of the gourmet trucks has been touting a specialty that is fairly universal and draws attention. Fish Lips Sushi Truck in Los Angeles obviously has a specialty with plenty of choices as does Crepes Bonaparte, also in Los Angeles, where you can start your day with the Wake-Me-Up Special crepe featuring egg, mozzarella, and pesto or stop by later for a Spicy Apple Bottoms crepe with cinnamon apples, caramel, and whipped cream. Meanwhile, Sam's Chowdermobile in San Francisco serves incredible clam chowder and also offers things like Maine lobster rolls. Not a bad lunch choice. The size of your operation and the popularity of your specialty determines how much you can put on your menu. It's not about quantity; it's about quality. Many trucks, like Los Angeles's famous Grilled Cheese truck, stick with a basic specialty and do it very well. This also holds true for running a cart or kiosk. You can be very creative within your setting.

A smaller venture only means thinking of unique ways to serve custom cuisine in a tighter space. Yes, you can certainly sell sushi from a cart or your own shrimp rolls from a kiosk. Keep in mind that while the food trucks are getting the press, the cart owners are keeping their costs way down. So don't be intimidated; there are plenty of options in the new street world of gourmet foods.

Ethnic Favorites

- Falafels
- Empanadas
- Egg Rolls
- Sushi
- Souvlaki
- Quesadillas
- Steamed Dumplings
- Kebobs

From Portland, Maine, down to Austin, Texas, and back up to Boston, ethnic food has changed the mobile food culture. Large markets are embracing authentic ethnic favorites while smaller markets are being introduced to new cuisines previously found in only a few establishments. "I had traveled a lot and missed things like the falafels and the street foods I had experienced in Europe. Selling falafels and kebobs in Market Square in Portsmouth, New Hampshire, was something new and they became very popular," says Michelle Lozuaway, who runs the Fresh Local truck in the small coastal town.

Much of the success found in ethnic fare emanates from the passion of the entrepreneurs. For example, the reason Curry Up Now is so popular in San Francisco is largely because the owners serve native foods from various parts of India, including a chicken tikka masala burrito. Another reason why Curry Up Now has long lines and may serve over 140 people an hour is because it changes its menu every day—not an easy task in the mobile food world. It is, however, a testament to the owners' desire to introduce native foods from all parts of India. If you're thinking Indian food and doing research, check out the India Jones Chow Truck in Los Angeles, which serves what it calls The Frankie, a roti roll-up with cilantro tamarind chutney, chopped onion and egg, and a choice of lamb, chicken, beef, shrimp, or veggies. Again, the owners are passionate about their foods.

Sometimes, it's all in the fillings, as in the Chairman Bao Truck in San Francisco that serves Chinese buns with fillings such as Chinese Spiced Duck Coalit or Mmmpanadas with eggs, cheese, bacon, or chorizo fillings for breakfast. Variations on a simple theme can sell very well, as evidenced by the Taco Truck in Hoboken, New Jersey, that features favorites like the Carnitas Michoacan Tacos, which are slow-braised sweet pork tacos seasoned with cilantro and onions.

Then there are the mixed ethnic options such as the Korean Mexican mix that made Kogi BBQ in Los Angeles the king of all food trucks and chef Roy Choi a foodie rock star. With some 50,000 followers, the famed vehicle serves Kogi Kimchi Quesadillas, Calamari Tacos, and other ethnic blends that combine Korean barbeque with homemade tortillas and other wrappings that have tastefully paved the way for the food truck revolution.

And if you can bring a new ethnic flavor to your town or city, by all means go for it. Yvonne's Jamaican Food Truck in Manhattan is doing just that with Jamaican favorites like curried goat or braised oxtail for only $6.50. On the other end of the country, Spencer on the Go brought French food such as escargot puffs, sweetbreads, and frog legs to the streets of San Francisco.

Desserts

- Ice Cream
- Cupcakes
- Donuts
- Brownies
- Cookies

Dessert trucks and carts carry those edible delights that make people smile. Whether it's cupcakes like the classic red velvet or the creative banana chocolate with salted caramel frosting from the Flirty Cupcakes truck in Chicago or the famous floats from Los Angeles's Lake Street Creamery, good dessert trucks or carts can create a brand name very quickly. Freshly made cupcakes, cookies, and brownies are easy to sell from a cart or a kiosk because customers can easily carry one or a bag of several. They are also easy to transport. In this case, your success is based largely on the freshness of your products, even more than on original flavors. Donuts may be a slightly tougher to market because Dunkin Donuts or Krispy Kreme are everywhere and hard to compete against.

Of course, ice cream is the definitive mobile dessert. We've seen the trucks for years, and hearing the music playing harkens most of us back to our childhood. In fact, Adria Shimada, who opened the Parfait Ice Cream truck in Seattle in 2009 as the first organic ice cream maker in the state, recalled that one of her reasons for opening an ice cream truck was to capture the good feelings from her youth. "I thought about America's inherent cultural nostalgia for the ice cream truck. Then I recalled my own fond memories of hearing the bells and whistles of the Good Humor man down the street, then getting this lovely treat. It was a warm and fuzzy experience," explains Shimada, who was determined to make homemade ice cream from scratch and now has a following of over 1,500 fans on Facebook for flavors like her Butter Toffee Crunch and fresh Mint Straccihella.

Smart Tip

Toppings: Because ice cream sales are very competitive, one way to stand out from the crowd is through innovative toppings. New York's Big Gay Ice Cream Truck, for example, offers toppings that include Trix Cereal, Pumpkin Butter, Ginger Syrup, Key Lime Curd, Fresh Berries and Saba, Nutella, and even Wasabi Pea Dust. Try getting that from Mr. Softee!

Like many dessert makers, Shimada has found that trying new and inventive flavors attracts a crowd, while simply making marvelous versions of standard favorites provides a mass audience.

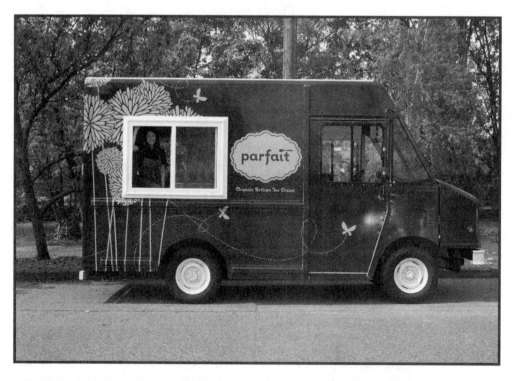

Adria Shimada peers out from her popular Parfait Ice Cream truck in Seattle, Washington.

While ice cream is certainly a fun food, the business needs to be taken just as seriously as that involving any other food. If you opt to make your own ice cream, understand that making it is a two-day, or more, process that needs to be repeated regularly and done very carefully. If you master it, you're past the first step to serving homemade ice cream. If not, buy manufactured ice cream and find creative and cost-effective ways of serving it—again, think toppings. It's also to your advantage to offer various sizes, choices of cones or cups, sundaes, and other options.

Because ice cream is scooped and then served, and scoop size can vary, you need to be extra careful when determining your costs. Your profit will be based on how many scoops you sell and what you need to charge per scoop and per topping. If you are serving homemade, organic fresh ice cream, you may need to charge more. After all, you have to buy each ingredient.

Along with scoopers and other equipment, your most important onboard item is your freezer. You'll want a chest freezer with an adjustable thermometer. No matter whether you are making ice cream or serving known brands and all sorts of popular pops for the kids, you will want to serve high-quality products and find good locations.

In many parts of the country, ice cream business drops off significantly between November and March. If you can plan carefully, you might be able to shift gears from a cart or truck to an indoor kiosk at a mall, hotel, or in a theater lobby by renting one well in advance for a few months. However, such locations may already be occupied. Another option is to cater kids' parties during the cold months or sell your ice cream in pints or larger quantities and deliver in your area. Adria of the Parafit Ice Cream truck is doing just that in Seattle. When it's too cold to take the truck out, she fills orders and delivers her homemade ice cream.

When selling ice cream, also consider selling gelato, sorbet, and other ice cream variations for the carb-conscious crowd.

> ## Tip...
>
> ## Smart Tip
> ### Don't Overdo It
> "I make more than 20 flavors of ice cream, but only offer about six at any given time," says Adria Shimada. The idea is to make life simple so that you only need to make a few flavors at a time. Then you can provide your customers with some choices but not so many that they stand there causing long lines to form while making a decision. Remember, unlike an ice cream shop, your counter space is very limited.

Beverages

- Soda
- Coffee
- Tea
- Hot Chocolate

manufacturers should be easily reachable and in many cases will sell you what you need or point you in the right direction so you can find their products nearby. Start with their websites. There are thousands of big companies to consider. There are also numerous small companies and niche providers that can supply you with a tremendous number of tasty options. From apples to zucchini, someone is ready with the food you need. As is the case when buying anything, compare prices along with quality as you shop

Local and Regional Suppliers

If you start looking locally, you will find food distributors in your area.

Regional suppliers like Cheney Brothers in the southeast (Cheneybrothers.com) and Smart and Final (smartandfinal.com) handling the West Coast can also be very helpful if you are in their area of distribution.

Greenmarkets and Farmers Markets

A very popular option for some of the new food carts and trucks hitting the streets is to sell the healthiest versions of the basic food truck favorites by seeking organic farms and greenmarkets. You'll have to charge a little more to cover the slightly higher costs, but you'll attract the health-conscious crowd, and that's a big demographic in some areas.

Food shopping is a huge endeavor for Adria Shimada, who looks for all organic products to use when making homemade ice cream for her Seattle food truck. "I get everything from a different distributor. Milk and cream come from a local certified organic dairy farm about 80 miles away, and I get eggs in another nearby town from another organic farm. All of my produce is real fresh produce, I don't use flavors or extracts. For my mint ice cream, I use real spearmint from a farm in Carnation, Washington," explains Shimada who scouted and tasted the food from many farms before finding her sources. Some deliver to her commercial kitchen, and others are found at farmer's markets in Seattle where farmers bring the wholesale quantities she needs.

Get to know area growers, talk to farmers and vendors at farmers' markets, and scout around carefully for whatever you need.

Food Cooperatives

When restaurateurs and/or mobile food owners order foods together in bulk quantities, they can save money. The larger the order, the better the discount. So if you can find some noncompetitive entrepreneurs, you can ask if they want to team up and place orders with you, which is how a food co-op is formed. A co-op is simply a group of individuals who come together for their mutual benefit, not unlike a credit union. You can look in your neighborhood for others interested in forming a co-op or, if you are interested in natural food co-ops (as well as finding plenty of information on co-ops), you can visit the Co-op Directory (coopdirectory.org).

Smart Tip

Tip...

If you are iPhone savvy, for $2.99 you can have the Locavore App that helps you find fresh, local, farm-to-table ingredients from a growing network of farmers' markets. The application also lets you know about foods in season in your area. For 99 cents you can get iFarmMarket, which lists more than 4,600 farmers' markets in the United States.

Shopping Clubs

BJ's Wholesale Club, Sam's Club, Costco, and other shopping clubs have become very popular in recent years as the idea of buying quality food in bulk has caught on. Restaurant owners shop at these clubs and so can you. Each requires a membership with an annual fee. You can then stock up on many items you need at good prices. Of course, you can also shop where the restaurant owners and their chefs shop—in places like Restaurant Depot and Jetro.

4

What's Off the Menu?

While it's true that the food is what lures most people into this particular industry, your truck, cart, trailer, bus, or kiosk is a key part your business equation. In essence, it's your partner. It is also what separates you from those brick-and-mortar restaurants, cafes, and snack bars that always seem to be nearby.

Along with mobility, the latest in technology provides you with a marvelous opportunity to compete with brick-and-mortar eateries. Smaller ovens, speedy convection ovens, mini-freezers, the latest in mobile generators, and a host of portable appliances make it possible to transport, cook, and serve foods almost anywhere. In addition, stainless steel counters and work stations, plus heavy duty cleaning products make it easier to meet health codes. You'll also find a wide selection of vehicles that are either built or retrofitted to your specifications. Gone are the days of struggling with a cart or truck that barely meets the needs of the food vendor. Today, you can hit the streets with the vehicle of your choice, or set up a state-of-the art kiosk in the busiest mall in town.You can also offer greater variety in food choices and grow a steady customer base thanks to high-tech communication tools.

There are advantages to being mobile. For example, besides not having to pay the high startup costs and monthly rent, you also do not need as many people on your payroll. And if a restaurant is not drawing a crowd, it is stuck in its location. You, on the other hand, can always pick up and move. Being mobile means finding locations you like. As for caterers, being mobile means you are not sitting with an empty catering hall during the slower months. Instead you can always create new themes and focus on holiday parties (for any occasion) rather than worrying about how you are going to pay your rent.

Of course the downside of mobility is the many local rules and regulations that can limit your opportunity to sell. In most regions of the United States and Canada, your sales success is also limited by inclement weather.

Sure there are pros and cons to going mobile, but if you are considering taking the plunge, then you need to focus on a vehicle (or kiosk) that meets your needs. Vehicle choice depend primarily on:

- Size and scope of your projected business endeavor
- Food or foods you plan to serve
- How much you are planning to invest in the business
- The area(s) in which you will be operating
- Your financial goals and expectations

Carts

"Carts are like cars, you can build a VW or a Mercedes Benz," says Mike Boyd from Cart King (cart-king.com), a major food cart seller that works with buyers to create the best cart for their individual needs. "The features you decide to include will depend on your needs and the state rules and regulations," adds Boyd.

Hot dog carts are typically pushcarts. They will have a grill, splashguard, hot and cold running water, two-basin sink, waste tank, plus a storage area for supplies and possibly an insulated storage area in which you can keep cold soda or bottled water.

Ice cream carts are typically pushcarts designed to hold ice cream vats, with a dipper well with running water, stainless steel pans or trays for toppings, display area, and storage compartments for cups, cones, etc. The latest in cold trays have replaced dry ice and remain cold during your sales day. They can be electrically charged during the off-hours.

"Food carts in the right locations can do $500 to $1,200 in business a day," notes Boyd, of the more successful cart owners.

Depending on your needs (and the local licensing requirements), you have carts that include:

- Stainless steal burners
- Propane tanks (and hook up) for power
- Power cord for indoor use or at fairs and other venues where electricity is available
- Display area(s)
- A stainless steel cooling compartment
- Three-basin stainless steel sink: for running water for food preparation, for washing your hands, and for cleaning utensils
- Hot and cold running water: uses a self-contained pump system with one tank for clean water tank and one for gray (or dirty) water.
- Hot water heater for coffee or espresso (or tea)
- Various storage areas
- A removable hitch for pulling by car or van
- Rear lights and blinker lights for towing
- Stainless steel counter, including a small cash register or cash box
- A heavy-duty canopy
- Heavy-duty handles for pushing
- Space for signage
- Large-capacity ice bin for holding cases of soda with ice or other cold products
- Display oven for pizza, pretzels, and knishes.
- Grill for heating foods
- Cold trays for ice cream

> **Tip...**
>
> **Smart Tip**
>
> Get a flattop grill. "Many carts today have flattop grills," says Mike Boyd of Cart King. "They make it easier for people to branch out and try new things like stir fry foods using a wok. They are also easy to heat and can be used to make multiple dishes like breakfast foods or hamburgers."

Ten Things to Consider When Buying a Cart

1. What features are included—do they meet your specific needs or not?
2. Ease of handling and comfort of handles or ease of hitching to your vehicle.
3. The weight of the cart. Is it too heavy to push? To tow?
4. How easy is it to secure everything so that nothing falls or breaks when moving
5. Does the cart require assembly when you buy it? How easy/difficult is it to assemble?
6. The wheels. Do they lock? Make sure they are sturdy and do not look worn.
7. The height and width. A narrower cart can squeeze in tight spaces—but may not have enough space to meet your needs.
8. Can you set it up and break it down easily?
9. Does the cart feel sturdy and well constructed?
10. And finally, consider the style and design. You want it to represent the theme of your business.

- Serving shelves
- Mechanical refrigeration
- Water softening system
- Water filtration system

Used Carts

A new six-by-three-foot food cart typically starts at about $4,000, but they can run up to $20,000 depending on the size, features, and quality. You can save a lot of money on a used cart. Just remember, you are putting your business on this vehicle, so make sure that it is in good condition. Like a used car, take it out for a spin or push, and make sure it is to your liking. Try shopping around. You can find used carts for $500 to $2,500, depending on wear and tear, size, and features. Look for a cart that was used to sell similar foods to those that you will be selling. After all, why convert a former ice cream cart to sell hot dogs? There are plenty of used hot dog carts available.

Kiosks

Typically a little more expensive than carts, ranging from $20,000 to $90,000 or more, food kiosks are generally used indoors in rented or leased spaces in malls, arenas, conference centers, hotels, airports, and similar locations. Larger, outdoor kiosks can be used at amusement parks.

It is important that you not only know the health codes and municipal requirements for food preparation and sales, but also the rules, regulations, and restrictions of the venue in which you will be selling. While kiosks generally do not have to deal with the limitations of the weather, you will probably have limitations imposed by the indoor location, especially hours of operation. If the mall stays open until 9 P.M., you obviously cannot stay open until 10 P.M. The same holds true if you are part of a food court. In addition, malls may specify that you have a design that fits in with their décor. They will also let you know what signage is and is not permitted, so make sure you meet the needs of the location before you buy, build, and/or retrofit a kiosk.

It can also be costly ($50,000+ per year) to lease space, depending on the location, the size of the venue, and terms of the lease.

A stand-alone kiosk is typically good for serving simple offerings such as pretzels, donuts, cupcakes, and other items that need not be heated. Coffee is the one hot product frequently sold in kiosks. To cook in a kiosk, you need a ventilation system so you do not have smoke billowing into an indoor facility. For this reason, kiosks serving cooked foods tend to be restricted to foods court where both ventilation and electricity are available. While your costs will be higher (because you are renting space in the venue), you can do upwards of $2,000 a day at a kiosk in a busy location. You may also consider franchising an express kiosk from one of many major food chains. (See Chapter 11 on franchising.)

Along with many of the features found in food carts (listed above), a kiosk may include:

- Extended, often lighted, counter space
- More display space

Beware!

Not unlike a brick-and-mortar business, the success of a kiosk depends largely on location, location, and location. Unlike carts, trucks, and busses, you are unable to pick up and move if business is slow. Therefore, it is important that you do not let yourself be lured into a lease or a "discount" rental price in a bad location. Make sure you scout carefully to see how much foot traffic the area actually has. Also see if you have any competition. Even if you are the only pretzel kiosk in the airline terminal or local mall, you should ask about having a clause in the lease that no other pretzel kiosk can open up while you are in there, at least not on the same floor.

▲

- Larger and lighted signage
- Refrigerated cases
- Actual roofs rather than canopies
- More cabinets and areas for supplies
- More elaborate design

Food Trucks

When buying a food truck, you have two specific issues to consider:

1. The truck itself
2. The food preparation portion of the truck

Despite the urge to start retrofitting a truck before you even test drive it, the need to have a vehicle that can serve you over the long haul is very important. No matter how good your food is, nobody gets to taste it if your truck is broken down somewhere in a tunnel.

Depending on the size of the truck, the equipment necessary, the retrofitting, and whether you are buying new or used, truck costs can run from $15,000 to more than $100,000. They can also take anywhere from a few weeks to six months (or more) to retrofit properly. Try to get a good estimate of time required from whomever you hire to design your truck, then add a month to the timeframe.

Obviously, the advantage to a new truck is that you get a warranty, have it designed to your liking, and built to meet local regulations from the start. Also, everything is brand new. Of course, the other side to the equation is that it will cost you a lot of money. If you do not have financial backers, this can delay making a profit.

As a result, many food truck owners work from used retrofitted trucks. If you decide to buy a used truck, you should have a mechanic that you trust inspect the vehicle carefully. Before even thinking about food, you want to make sure the truck is in good shape to travel and carry your equipment on a daily basis. Kim Ima, owner of the Treats Truck of New York, which sells cookies, brownies, and other baked goods, found a used vehicle for sale on eBay in the fall 2006 and bought it for less than $20,000. Laurent Katgely, who owns the San Francisco French restaurant Chez Spencer, opened a food-truck business called Spencer on the Go after buying a former burrito truck for $15,000. In fact, most of the food truck owners interviewed for this book purchased used trucks to start their businesses.

When buying a truck, you will need to consider typical truck issues, such as how well the truck handles, how easy it is to maneuver and whether it can accommodate the

Three Key Concerns for Used Truck Buyers

1. *The Engine.* Have it checked out by a licensed mechanic

2. *Space Issues.* Measure to make sure not only your equipment will fit, but that there will be sufficient room for one or two people to work comfortably.

3. *Is it Cost-Effective?* A used truck, retrofitted to meet you needs and health code regulations, should cost significantly less than a new truck.

weight of the necessary equipment. Keep in mind that a heavier truck (typically over 26,000 pounds) will also require the driver to have a commercial truck driver's license.

Used trucks may come with some wear and tear, so you will need to check the truck out carefully. Make sure that everything works, from the sinks and freezers to the headlights and sound system, if there is one.

What to consider when buying a food truck.

- Does the truck handle well? Make sure the truck does not overwhelm you and that it is easy to maneuver.
- Is it easy to see behind you and alongside of you from the mirrors?
- Is there enough room to fit the equipment you want into the truck and still maneuver comfortably inside?
- Is the price within your budget? Are there financing options?
- What is the weight of the truck? A heavier truck (typically over 26,000 pounds) will usually require a commercial (truck) drivers license.

When buying a used truck:

- Check the year, model, and make of the vehicle as well as the mileage. You want to make sure you can find parts if necessary. You also don't want a truck that has significant mileage.
- Make sure the engine and all parts are in good condition
- Determine if the truck is retrofitted to meet your needs and how much will need to be changed.
- What is the condition of the equipment? How much needs to be replaced? (Hint, check to see that everything works, from the headlights and the radio to the sinks and food warmers.)

- Is there enough room to meet your specific equipment needs?

In addition to many of the features found in food carts, trucks may also include:

- Larger refrigerators and/or freezers
- More power through propane or a generator
- Additional food service or preparation equipment
- Additional cabinet and supply space
- Side serving windows and countertops

When searching for a truck, you might consider buying an inexpensive van, former postal truck, or a similar nonfood-related vehicle. A number of food truck owners have done this. The truck is retrofitted, which typically means removing any seats except those in the front, changing the flooring to something that is very easy to clean (and not slippery), and building a counter and window in the side of the vehicle. You will also need to install power via propane tanks or a generator.

FYI

Whether you plan to cook on your truck, bus, or attached trailer, you must have a hood/fan system with a fire suppression device. If you are using gas, you must also include an automatic gas shutoff with the hood system. This equipment can be costly to install and maintain, so an off-site commercial kitchen, which comes with such equipment, can be a better choice. In fact, some cities require you to cook in an off-site commercial kitchen.

Mobile Catering Trucks

Beware!
One of the biggest mistakes food truck owners make is overloading their vehicle. Trucks can only carry so much weight before they start having maintenance problems. Look for a truck that can accommodate all that you require. Your truck should be able to handle at least 15,000 pounds as the gross vehicle weight.

Mobile catering trucks are those hired to provide food for a party or gathering at a location of the client's choice. If your catering business is primarily transporting food and not serving it, you face less stringent requirements then if you are preparing and serving food. Along with the concerns about purchasing a good quality vehicle, you need to purchase the right truck for what you do. If transporting food from your kitchen to the location of the party or event is your number-one concern, then you need to focus on square footage, shelving, and ability to secure everything you are carrying. Of course

you may need refrigerators, freezers, and/
or warmers. If you are not serving from
the truck, sinks and serving areas are not
necessary, minimizing some costs.

Conversely, if you are actually cooking
on site, you will need food preparation
permits and licensing. Again, you have to
determine if legally you can cook on board
your vehicle in your town or city. If you
cannot, your other option is to bring grills
and other equipment and cook in designated
areas, such as places where barbecuing is
allowed. More on mobile catering is found in Chapter 8.

A typical mobile kitchen includes:

Smart Tip

Measure all equipment
carefully. You only have
so much room in any vehicle or
kiosk. Your designer can help you
determine what fits, but you may
need to add equipment or make
changes. Measure, measure,
measure.

- Cooking equipment with an exhaust hood
- Refrigerator
- Utensil and hand-washing sinks with hot and cold running water
- Service windows
- Stainless steel counters
- Roof windows with aluminum screens
- Prep tables and/or counters
- Multiple storage counters/sinks
- Propane tanks
- Emergency exit

Bustaurants

Bustaurants are new. World Food and Le Truc are among the originals, breaking
new ground and ruffling some feathers. To buy a Greyhound or a double-decker bus
and retrofit it as a restaurant can cost upwards of $250,000. The concept of using the
upper deck or part of the vehicle as a dining area is unknown in most towns, cities, and
counties, forcing legislators to write new rules. Meanwhile, you will be subject to the
same health department licensing rules and regulations of food trucks.

The novelty of the bustaurant is eating onboard. To accentuate that novelty,
themes are also part of the "charm" of this new dining experience. Essentially anything
you could put in a cart or truck can fit into a bus—and more—depending on local rules

and regulations. You need to calculate and measure the space for actual dining, which means tables and chairs, but the number of diners you can have may be dictated by fire department regulations.

While those with a lot of capital can consider the bustaurant as an exciting venture, there are some issues you have to deal with.

- Their success is unproven. Because they are so new, it is not clear if they are a passing fad (literally) or here to stay.
- They require a driver or drivers that are comfortable handling a vehicle of this size and licensed to do so.
- There will certainly be parking issues. San Francisco's Le Truc has been met with protests. Local authorities tend not to want busses parking all over town.
- The cost of maintaining a bus is significant.
- While some are greener than others, running on bio diesel, many environmentalists are not thrilled with the idea of having more busses on their city streets.

In high tourist areas, bustaurants seem to be popular thus far. They may become the next generation of mobile dining or remain as a novelty—time will tell. Most newcomers to the industry would be advised to follow them (literally if possible) to see how they do before jumping on board.

On the bright side, in many cities you would be among the first to have such a large mobile dining facility. While municipalities typically frown upon food preparation and even serving food while on the move, you can plot out an itinerary that has a different course at each of a few locations. You can also pick up customers and drive around before and after the dinner is served. Why not have your customers transported from the hustle and bustle of downtown to a romantic location, serve a romantic dinner, and then bring them back? With the right theme, atmosphere, and promotion, a bustaurant can be a unique and profitable business. Look at World Fare and Le Truc. But, be forewarned, it is a costly adventure.

Retrofitting

Adria's Parfait Ice Cream truck in Seattle was bought used from someone in Michigan who ran it as a traditional ice cream truck, selling packaged products. Adria makes homemade ice cream and had to customize the truck to meet Seattle health codes because she was actually scooping the ice cream herself, which is considered food preparation. "An ice cream truck or a cart selling packaged products doesn't need the same equipment, such as a hand sink on the truck, so my truck had to have sinks installed to meet the regulations," explains Adria.

Like most entrepreneurs, she carefully considered what she would need for her small truck and made a list. Designers typically work from the list you provide for retrofitting and make recommendations based on what you need in order to meet health codes. They can also help you with size and space issues, which are trickier than you might think.

Plan Carefully—Have a Design in Mind

Wouldn't you like to design your kitchen from scratch? Well here's your chance, sort of. From a cart to a bustaurant, you need to map out exactly what you need and where it will be located in order to prepare and/or serve customers efficiently. You have no time to be looking around for things while a line forms out front. The larger the vehicle and/or the more foods you are selling, the more carefully you have to review your floor plan. Rule of thumb says keep it simple when starting out by serving only a few items or make one item (i.e., cupcakes or ice cream) and make it very well, with variations on the theme.

"We looked at what we physically needed to do on our truck from the starting point to the end point, and exactly what happens in-between," explains Greg Anson from EVOL Foods. "We literally mimicked the motions of what people are going to

Phil Anson's interior plan for his EVOL Foods Burrito trailer.

do in the flow of getting the product from freezer into the ovens, out of the ovens, and to the customers. It was like choreographing a motion study," says Anson, who, like a choreographer, refined it again and again.

Your plan, whether created by hand or on a computer program, should outline the specific equipment you need and the easiest way to move around efficiently, including the best places to put everything you need to heat and serve food quickly. For example, if you are selling pizza, you need a pizza oven, three-compartment sink, hot water system, beverage cooler, freezer, and prep fridges all mounted properly. You want sufficient counterpace, a multitiered heated display case, room for your cash register, a place for toppings, and storage for paper goods, cleaning supplies, and anything else you need to bring along, plus a fire extinguisher and a propane fuel system to power most of the above. You also need proper ventilation, a serving window, and more.

FYI

There are many cart, truck, and kiosk designers. Asking other mobile food vendors, doing a search on Google, or checking the resources in the back of this book can provide names of places. Many outfitters will take care of permits, insurance, and maintenance; and some include POS technology. Ask what is offered before selecting someone to be your designer.

Once you have worked with a designer to retro fit the truck, you will need to map out how someone will take a slice from a heated display, add toppings, heat a slice or individual pizza, get the customer's drink (if you also serve drinks), take the heated slice, serve it to the customer, and collect the money all in a fluid motion. You want to have a smooth system in place to avoid mishaps on the truck.

Buying or Renting

Depending on the equipment and the size, a new food truck could cost you more than $100,000. Conversely, renting a truck will cost you about $3,000 a month (depending on the size and condition of the vehicle.) The obvious advantage of renting is the cost saving. As is typically the case, the downside of renting is that you cannot sell the truck one day. You are also held to the terms of the rental agreement. Another option is to start a business with a rented vehicle, see how it goes, and possibly buy the vehicle once you are familiar with it and have determined that you like being part of the mobile food business. Look for rentals with an option to buy.

Most mobile food business owners agree that establishing a system is vital. To do this effectively the cart, kiosk, truck, or bus needs to be built and set up to your liking. The importance of working closely with your designer cannot be overstated. It can be very costly (and a waste of your time) to redo the infrastructure of your retrofitted vehicle once it is completed.

If you are buying an existing vehicle for the same usage, perhaps selling espresso just like the previous owner, it is advantageous to study how he ran the show. Of course, you may still want to make some minor changes to suit your needs.

Where Do Food Trucks and Carts Sleep?

Food kiosks typically stay at one location for the duration of the lease. As an owner, you need to make sure everything is carefully shut down at the end of the day. Often trailers shut down and remain at a location if it is permitted. For carts, trucks, and busses, however, the situation is usually different. Many cities require that a mobile food vehicle be parked in a health department–approved commissary parking location for both health and safety reasons. You will, therefore, have to find such a facility in your area. Rates vary from several hundred dollars per month to upwards of $1,000,

Electrical Equipment

According to West Coast Catering, a company that sells catering trucks, electrical equipment in a food truck or mobile catering truck may include:

- ○ Interior fluorescent light fixtures with approved covers
- ○ Exterior light fixtures installed on service doors
- ○ Two-speed electrical fans in the exhaust hood
- ○ Electric water heater
- ○ 48-, 60-, 72-inch refrigerator
- ○ 110v electrical outlets
- ○ Electric generator: 2000 or 3000 watt output (quiet model)
- ○ 12-volt battery back-up system with battery charger
- ○ 15 amp. fuse block for fans and light fixtures

depending on the local authority, the size of the vehicle, and what else is included besides just the parking. Facilities vary significantly. Some parking locations wash vehicles and sell fuel or propane. Many will let you use electricity to charge your equipment. Ask if there is a fee or it is included in your rental agreement.

It is also important to find parking that you consider safe. Many commissaries have security cameras and even someone on duty 24/7. You also want to know about the access if you plan to bring your vehicle back at off-hours. such as after serving the late night crowd leaving a ballgame at midnight or the nightclub crowd leaving the local hot spot at 3 A.M. A commissary that is not far from your commercial kitchen, if you are using one, is also a plus. Sometimes the same company provides both a kitchen and vehicle parking, though typically not in the same location.

Once again, bustaurants are charting a new course. Indoor commissaries often do not have the room for parking large vehicles. You may need to find outdoor parking lots that are deemed satisfactory by the Department of Health, so this issue is important to investigate before starting a bustaurant.

Taking Care of Your Vehicle

Nobody wants to miss a day of work because of a flat tire or engine trouble, especially if you are in the mobile food industry where your inventory is also at risk of being wasted.

Because your wheels are almost as important as your menu, although less tasty, you need to have regular check-ups scheduled for your vehicle. If not for your own good, you will need to do this to appease the people handing out your permits and renewing your licenses. Remember, vehicle inspection counts for a lot in this business.

Routine maintenance not withstanding, it is to your advantage to take a course in vehicle maintenance. It is also your responsibility to keep the guidebook that comes with a new vehicle or at least check the manufacturer's website for additional information about a used vehicle. Chevy, for example, has troubleshooting information online, as do most other vehicle manufacturers.

To play it safe, you or your driver must be aware of the condition of the truck. The wear and tear of carrying heavy equipment on a daily basis can take its toll on your vehicle. Many food and mobile catering truck owners are so concerned about the food end of the business that they neglect their vehicles. Plenty of stories abound of those bad days when truck owners learned that the alternator did not work, the battery died (never depend on the battery to power food equipment), or the gas gauge was on empty or a bit below before you almost reached your destination.

Therefore, you must:

- Check recall announcements. Some recalls are more critical than others for keeping the truck in service. You can visit www.AutoRecalls.us for recall information.
- Pay attention to all engine warning lights on the dashboard and never ignore one that is lit.
- Keep an eye on the gas gauge.
- Check the engine oil frequently.
- Make sure all lights are working.
- Make sure the fuel tank is not leaking.
- Make sure your spark plugs are not worn.
- Make sure all connections in the engine are not loose or eroding.
- Check your tire pressure often.
- Make sure windshield wipers are working, and change the blades if they are getting worn down.
- If you hear a noise while driving and all food equipment is off, pull over, stop, and shut the vehicle off. When you start up again (assuming you can start up again), check under the hood if the sound continues to see if you can tell where it is coming from. Unless you have taken a troubleshooting course and know what to do, have the engine looked at by a mechanic as soon as possible.

Your commissary may offer some help with an available mechanic. If not, find someone you can trust. Also keep in mind that some national parts chains offer free diagnostic testing. Such testing can identify a problem.

Cart owners should not think this section is only for larger vehicles. While you will not have engine problems to worry about, wheels need to be in good shape at all times. Lights on the back of a vehicle being pulled are also supposed to work. In short, take the time to examine the cart carefully and make sure that all working parts are in good order. You will also very likely be required to park your cart in a specified area. In some cities, like New York, there are trucks that can be rented which take several carts at the end of

Smart Tip

A GPS can be helpful, especially when driving a catering truck and looking for a client's location. In addition to directions, a GPS can help you find your way to the nearest service station or garage, which can be a lifesaver if you are in need of gas or repairs in the middle of your busy day.

a working day and transport all of them to a garage where they will be safe and sound overnight. Remember, your business is riding on your cart, so take good care of it.

Equipping Artisan Ice Cream Trucks in New York City

In 2008 the first two Van Leeuwen Artisan Ice Cream trucks hit the streets of New York City. Today there are six trucks selling everything from finest quality chocolate and vanilla ice cream to mint chip, cinnamon, hazelnut, and red currents blended with fresh cream.

The original vehicles were 1988 Chevrolet step vans. "We use plate freezers that plug in and charge up overnight, so they don't need to be running during the day. This is great for the environment but also great because it keeps our trucks nice and quiet. We use small clean-air generators to run the lights, cash register, and coffee equipment on our newer trucks. Also on our new coffee/ice cream trucks we have Mirage Veloce espresso machines. These are custom-built by hand in the Netherlands by Kees Van der Westen and are the only ones of their kind in New York City," explains Laura O'Neill, co-owner of the business with her husband Ben Van Leeuwen and his brother Pete Van Leeuwen.

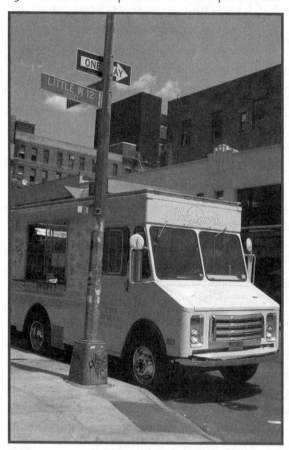

One of the Van Leeuwen Artisan Ice Cream Trucks parked in New York City, as photographed by co-owner Laura O'Neill.

Can I Park Here?
Licenses, Regulations, and Points of Sales

Before you finish putting your menu together, building your perfectly retrofitted cart or truck, setting up your kiosk or hitting the road on a fabulous bustaurant, you need to get your licensing in order. While that's not one of the more exciting aspects of your entrepreneurial pursuit, it's one of the most important. It is, in fact, the overall commitment to more stringent health codes and sanitary regulations that have paved the way for food vehicles to generate such a mass following. The knock against food carts and trucks has long been that they were neither clean nor sanitary. Now, as that widespread perception changes, foodies and nonfoodies alike can enjoy their fare with confidence that those running the business are doing their utmost to meet, and surpass, sanitary requirements.

Licenses and Permits

It would probably take several volumes to list and explain the numerous permits and licensing requirements because each state as well as most cities and even counties have their own. However, there are many universal concerns that need to be addressed. Typically, your local department of health will have the information you need. Therefore, you can get started by looking up the local health department online or in your local Yellow Pages and calling to inquire about the necessary requirements.

The state or city will have specific requirements that must be met depending on your mode of operation. If you are selling prepackaged foods, you are not considered a food handler and may have less stringent requirements than if you are actually preparing foods or even scooping ice cream. As long as food is unwrapped, you are typically considered to be a food handler and must meet specific regulations. While your cart or truck designer will not know the nuances of each city's requirements, they can usually help you meet health standards. Before you can hit the road, health inspectors will inspect your vehicle. What are inspectors actually looking for? In Washington, D.C., for example, an inspection is conducted to verify the following:

- Proof of ownership, proper identification, and license (of the vehicle)
- Proof of District-issued Food Manager Identification Card
- Food purchase record storage and record keeping
- Depot, commissary, or service support facility meets vending unit operation needs
- Copy of license for the service support facility and/or a recent inspection report be presented.

Food vehicles are typically inspected at least once a year by a health department inspector, sometimes randomly. The

FYI

There are nearly 20,000 separate licensing jurisdictions in the United States. Each has its own particular licensing requirements. Getting in touch with the right one(s) and finding out exactly what forms you need and how to submit them can be time consuming and tedious—but, it's part of business. Dedicate at least three days to locating and filling out forms.

inspector checks to see how food is stored so that it does not spoil and that it is kept at the proper temperature. All food equipment as well as sinks and water supplies are checked. Commercial kitchens and garages in which food vehicles are kept are also inspected frequently and can be given high fines if they do not meet health and fire codes. Some have been shut down because of too many violations. Likewise, trucks and carts have lost their licenses over repeated violations.

Take New York City

One of the owners or partners of the intended food vehicle must have a mobile food-vending license with a photo ID badge. Once that is received, a Mobile Food Vending (MFV) Unit Permit is issued to the individual or business that wants to prepare and sell food from a mobile vehicle. After an inspector from the Department of Health and Mental Hygiene (DOHMH) conducts an inspection of the vehicle and it passes, the permit is affixed to the vehicle.

According to the NYC DOHMH, the number of MFV Unit Permits that may be issued for use on public space is limited by law. At present there is a very long waiting list, so getting a permit can take years. Those interested in obtaining a public space permit may only apply for one when DOHMH notifies them that their name has come up.

To work at street fairs or special events, people need to apply for a Temporary Food Service Establishment permit. A Restricted Area MFV unit permit can also be obtained to operate on private property or in a commercially zoned area.

Keep in mind that permits need to be renewed. Renewal applications are mailed to the last known address of the permit holder as the permit nears expiration, so remember to update your address should you move.

One way entrepreneurs have gotten around the problem of being unable to get a license from the city is by teaming up with those who already have licenses and including them in their business. They also may rent vehicles from those with licenses, which is technically illegal, but not typically enforced. Buying a license on the black market can get you arrested. Needless to say, nobody talks very much about licenses in the Big Apple.

⚠ Beware!

A typical food cart owner in New York City paid $433 in fines in 2009. Common fines (and many of these pertain to other cities as well) include being too far from the curb, too close to a building entrance, not offering a customer receipt, vending in a bus stop, and not conspicuously displaying the license on the vehicle. Similar laws pertain to truck and trailer owners, and violations are also handed out. Keep in mind that some cities are more lenient regarding street food rules than others. New York City averages 59,000 violations to cart owners a year.

Playing It Safe

To be on the safe side, it is highly recommended that you check with the proper regulating agencies in your area regarding specific requirements for your vehicle. You should also get into the habit of being as sanitary as possible from the planning stages forward. For example, food preparers today are required to wear disposable food preparation gloves—you can buy a box of 500 for less than $15 on Amazon.com. Foods should be wrapped or kept in sealed containers unless they are being heated or served. Sauces should be served in individual portions in disposable containers or in pour squeeze bottles. All foods that require refrigeration should be stored at proper temperatures. Proper refrigeration is extremely important because the last thing you want is to serve food that has gone bad. A bad reputation and/or lawsuit can ruin your business. Your freezer should be enclosed with an approved thermometer readable from outside the unit. In a truck or trailer, you are also required to have an adequate ventilation and/or air conditioning system that is able to maintain the interior ambient temperature within the proper temperature range of the refrigeration equipment.

As for retrofitting your vehicle, you'll want to start with the must-haves to meet inspection requirements in your municipality. You'll want to make sure that everything retrofitted into your vehicle is easily washable, from the floors to the walls to the preparation and serving areas. Use smooth, easily cleanable surfaces. This is why stainless steel is popular for equipment and commercial grade linoleum for floors. Also, doors and garbage can covers (all covers, for that matter) need to be tight fitting. Trash receptacles need to be lined with proper trash bags. From major food preparation equipment down to proper dispensers for napkins, stirrers, and plastic utensils, you need to address everything in the vehicle or kiosk from the safest, most sanitary perspective possible. The department of health in your area will spell all of this out in detail.

Other things health departments frown upon include:

- Rust
- Wood surfaces
- Jagged or sharp edges
- Anything that is obstructed from cleaning
- Uncovered plastic utensils for customers
- Lack of splash guards around hand-washing sinks

Smart Tip

Tip...

Don't leave cracks or crevices when outlining your truck design. The more you can streamline the truck so that insects or vermin have no dark areas in which to hide, the better off you will be. Counters should be continuous. and storage should go to the floor. In fact, light colors are advised, and in some cities/counties they are mandatory.

If you are operating a full kitchen on your vehicle, you will have additional state and/or local requirements. Most retrofitters and kiosk, cart, and truck sellers can help you through the process. Bustaurants essentially follow the rules for trucks and will very likely have new health regulations as they become more popular.

Application Process Prerequisites

Of course, before you can even apply for most licenses, you need to have your own information readily available. While local authorities vary in what they require, you will typically need to provide your:

- Mailing address and proof of address
- LLC, partnership, or a stamped copy of corporation papers
- Social security number or tax identification number
- Valid photo ID
- Valid driver's license (for at least one person involved in the business)
- A list of all operators of the vehicle
- State certificate of sales tax
- Business license(s) and/or certificates as required by state, city, or county

These are some of the basics that may be required. Double- and triple-check with the licensing authority before showing up without one of the many necessary documents. In some areas, you may need to get a license or permit from other agencies, such as environmental agencies or local fire inspectors, particularly if you are operating a mobile kitchen.

Business Permits

Don't forget that with all the food service permits and meeting the stringent health requirements, you may also need to get the necessary business licenses in your city or county. City hall or the county clerk's office can usually point you in the right direction. Fees for business licenses are generally under $100. You can also go to your local city hall website to get appropriate licensing information. If you are doing business under the name of the truck or company, you will need a DBA (Doing Business As) certificate. This indicates that legally you are doing business under a fictitious name.

In addition, in most states business owners are required to register their business with a state tax agency and apply for certain tax permits as a seller. You may need to apply for a state sales tax permit. Consult your local tax office or check the IRS website (irs.gov). And if you are hiring employees, make sure to get an Employer Identification Number or EIN (aka a federal tax ID). The nine-digit EIN is important because it allows you to identify your business on government forms and official documents. Your federal tax ID not only makes the folks at the IRS happy when you file tax returns but also can be used in place of your personal Social Security number when you need to show business identification, thus keeping your SS number off of a lot of forms. Even if you are not hiring employees, you will need an EIN number if you have incorporated. The IRS makes it very easy to apply for EIN numbers and explains what you need to do on its website irs.gov.

> **Beware!**
> It is of the utmost importance that if you have any employees, you keep records of them on the books and stick to the schedule of tax withholding payments. After all the time and effort you have put into opening your food business, you would hate to be shut down because the IRS finds out that you are hiring people and not following the tax laws for your employees.

While most mobile food businesses are not incorporated, one reason to consider incorporating is to protect yourself personally from liability. If someone gets sick or injured and decides to sue you, she can sue the corporation and not go after your personal assets. While you may not be completely protected, it does put a layer of separation between you and your business. Incorporation primarily means filing a lot of papers and maintaining more stringent records. USA.Gov has plenty of information on incorporating (usa.gov/Business/Incorporate.shtml) as does Nolo.com (nolo. com) and the Company Corporation (incorporate.com). Of course you should first consult with your attorney to see if such a move, or forming a LLC (Limited Liability Company), is right for your business.

Vehicle Licensing

Don't forget that vehicle permits and inspections are vital to your business. Food not withstanding, if you're driving a vehicle you will need to have proper vehicle registration. Carts and trailers may also need to be registered. Make sure you check with the motor vehicle department to find out exactly what you need in your area, and stay on top of renewals. In addition, broken tail lights and other such problems need to be addressed prior to an inspection.

You need to have commercial plates on your vehicle but in most cities and states you only need a commercial driver's license if you are operating a vehicle over 26,000 pounds. Check the vehicle weight requirements in your state. Visit the Federal Motor Carrier Safety License Administration (fmcsa.dot.gov) for more information.

Zoning, Parking, and Other Considerations

Towns, cities, and counties have zoning restrictions, designating commercial and noncommercial zones. While you may be mobile, you can't park just anywhere. Most areas limit food trucks, trailers, busses, and carts to specific locations. A list of where you can and cannot park should be available from the county clerk—be persistent because you want to avoid parking tickets. In some places, you may also have to adhere to two-hour parking restrictions and (believe it or not) pay for parking meters—yes, even carts. Having to adhere to strict parking rules and being subject to parking violations is one headache kiosk owners can avoid.

Try not to dodge the local police because they will catch on and make your life more difficult. It's advisable to stay within the guidelines and befriend local authorities (give a cop a donut—just kidding!). However, if you play fair and establish a good rapport, when you do accidentally park in the wrong place or overstay your welcome, they may be more lenient.

Also be careful to park as close to the curb as possible—and never double park. You should also find out about other, lesser-known parking restrictions. Contact your local motor vehicle department or look for a local website online with city or town ordinances. For example, some municipalities have laws stating that a food truck or cart cannot park within a school zone or within X blocks from a school during school hours.

Then there are the store and restaurant owners that do not like your presence and will call the cops on you if you get too close to their businesses. At local town meetings these business owners (paying property taxes) are often heard from before food truck owners. In fact, Raleigh, North Carolina, banned food trucks from parking on the city's streets! Politicians in other cities, such as Los Angeles (as of the writing of this book), are proposing specific food truck parking areas (like those for taxis), limiting the food trucks to certain locations.

Restaurant owners obviously do not want competition in front of their establishment. Of course, most food truck drivers get it and don't want to make trouble. Scott Baitinger of the Streetza pizza truck, in Milwaukee, notes that there are not many stringent parking requirements in that city for food trucks as of yet, but says he simply would not park within 500 feet of a pizza parlor. Other food truck owners have made similar statements. Of course, the battles continue. In Chicago Holly Sjo, owner of the Cupcake Counter, a small brick-and-mortar shop, called the police when she spotted the popular Flirty Cupcakes truck parked too close to her business. Chicago city ordinances prohibit parking within "200 feet of a restaurant and 100 feet of a business offering a similar service." It can lead to a ticket. Some business owners

No Wine, No Beer

You cannot sell alcohol from a mobile food vehicle. If you try to do so, you can lose your license. What you can do is look for a location for food sales within a reasonable (and allowable) distance of a neighborhood bar selling alcohol and promote each other.

As for an indoor kiosk, you'll have to consult your local laws as they may allow the sale of alcohol in some counties. In Pennsylvania, for example, automated wine kiosks drew a lot of attention when introduced in the summer of 2010.

complain that food trucks accumulate parking tickets and just write them off as a business expense. While this is not the norm, trucks that are piling up tickets can make more trouble for everyone as city officials and business owners then work for stricter laws. In fact, it has been proposed in some areas that a certain number of tickets could result in the truck owner having his license suspended.

On the other hand, as Baitinger points out, his truck has gained a following and owners of some businesses such as nightclubs want the truck nearby to draw business to their establishment. As food trucks gain their own following, business owners continue to both hate and love them, depending on the impact—or potential impact—to their businesses. A popular, well-placed food truck can be useful by drawing customers to the right establishment.

Smart Tip

Tip...

If you team up with a noncompetitive business owner, you can both benefit by drawing business to each other. Look for someone who would benefit from your demographic audience and visa versa. Then come up with a cooperative marketing idea.

Location, Location, Location

Your locations will play a major factor in your success. Your decisions on where to park for business purposes will depend on several key factors. First, you have to consider where you are allowed to park by law. Next, you want to ask yourself where in those areas can you find the customers that would like your foods and/or beverages. You also want to consider the prime hours for each potential location and, of course, the competition. Keep in mind that even if you've found the perfect lunch location on the map and you are allowed to park there, you may also find 19 other food carts and trucks lining the streets.

As more food trucks appear on the streets of major cities like New York, Los Angles, and San Francisco, it becomes much more difficult to find prime locations. Add in the fact that there will be business owners who do not want you parking near their establishments, and it can be a major challenge coming up with good places to do business.

Twitter has become a very useful tool for communicating with your foodie fans. They can guide you to where they are waiting. However, as they do so, they may also unintentionally guide your competitors to the same location. Twitter has been most effective at letting foodies know that their favorite truck is in its usual place. Your goal should be, as it is for most mobile food vendors, to find a few regular locations, or in the case of some vehicles such as Mmmpanadas in Texas, one prime location. However, this is not as easy as it sounds. So what are food cart and truck drivers to do?

Some places to consider parking are:

- *Office parks.* Find out if food trucks are allowed to park and during what hours. If you are lucky enough to find an office park without much competition, stake a claim, or get a permit (if necessary) from the renting or leasing company to park there regularly. Breakfast and lunch hours should be your primary time slots.

- *Empty lots.* If you can find out who owns the property, make an offer to pay to park there on a regular basis. You can propose a flat daily rate, a percentage of your sales, or both. Such an agreement can benefit both parties and give you a chance to establish yourself. Of course you need to find a lot where there is enough foot traffic to make it worthwhile.

- *Shopping districts or malls.* You may or may not be allowed to park on a public street alongside the stores. Public streets are governed by local traffic laws. That being said, storeowners have a lot of say. Know your local ordinances. You may, however, be able to park near the parking lots or on an adjacent corner to a mall entrance. Malls will likely require you to have a permit to park on their property—inquire within the mall. Established shopping areas may have little room for you to park, but newer areas, recently opened for business, may give you an opportunity. You may, however, have some growing pains along with the storeowners.

- *Popular tourist locations.* The tourist crowd is often a great demographic. However, the competition can be fierce near well-known attractions. Sure, you will find food carts around Central Park in New York City, but many have established themselves in specific locations, making it nearly impossible to break into their territory. In some cases, you may need to pay for the privilege of parking at a prime tourist attraction, and it can be pricey. The CupCakeStop owners pay several thousand dollars a month to park at the popular South Street Seaport in lower Manhattan.

You can also look for the opening of a new museum, gallery, theater, arena, visitor's center, or anyplace that has just been added to the list of must-see places in your city.

- *Sports venues.* You may need permits to get close to an arena or stadium. However, if there is street parking for ticket holders, you can usually try to get on a street or a major roadway leading to or from the facility. Know which teams play where, and get a schedule in advance so you don't find yourself outside a football stadium in May.

- *Festivals and events.* "We take the truck to local events like Market Square Day, which brings in like 80,000 people, which is a lot for a town of 25,000," says Michelle Lozuaway of Fresh Local in Portsmouth, New Hampshire.

  "We look on an annual calendar and plan about a year in advance to go to major events," says Phil Anson of EVOL Burritos. "We're small, so we do four or five events per year, like the Natural Product Expo West in Anaheim in March (a major trade show) or the Summer and Winter X-Games. Most festivals have websites so that you can find out about leasing a space well in advance. If you check a local event calendar or go to the website for a current or recent annual festival, you will usually be able to find out the date for next year and get a contact number."

- *Conferences and conventions.* As is the case with festivals, if they are annual events, they are planned well in advance. Get to know where they are staged and lease your space well in advance or find a place on a public street that leads to the conference or convention center.

- *Parks and beaches.* You need permits to park in a park or on beach property. Check with the local parks commission to see if you can get such a permit and at what cost. Carts may have the upper hand here because they take up less space. One of the six Van Leeuwen Artisan Ice Cream trucks in New York City is parked by the former Tavern on the Green restaurant location in Central Park, thanks to a parks department permit and the okay by the owners of the restaurant property.

- *Bus and train stations.* If there is room, by all means consider these as busy locations where people may be hungry. Again, you have to know where you can park, so inquire. Also, get an idea of which hours will see the most foot traffic.

- *College campuses.* Off campus, public streets may be good for parking. However, unless it is a commuter school, you may not have a lot of traffic. To get on campus for a few hours a day, you need to get a permit from the school, and that may be difficult depending on the institution and its policies. If nothing else, you may be able to secure a spot when there are major school events, such as football or basketball games.

- *The business district.* Serving lunch in the middle of a busy business area can be terrific. However, in some cities, like New York, it's next to impossible to just slip into the mix without angering the competition (and you don't want to do that). Again, look for developing areas. Read about companies moving downtown or uptown or to a part of town that is now being built up or re-zoned for commercial use. Try to stake a claim in an up-and-coming area. You may struggle at first, as do many new businesses, but in time you may be the king of the hill.

Beware!

If you find a marvelous location in a popular food truck/cart town and over a number of days see no other food vehicles, chances are there is a reason. Sometimes things are too good to be true. Check this location out carefully before settling in. Chances are you can't legally park there, so be ready to move quickly.

Learning all about parking rules and regulations in your city and finding the best potential locations for your business takes due diligence. Even once you have found a few locations to your liking, keep on scouting around. Parking rules and regulations, as well as local ordinances, change often, so a good location one month may be gone the next. Also, note that as the seasons change, some locations become less viable, such as your great spot by the beaches on the Jersey shore, which will not be so great in the fall or winter months. So come up with other plans.

Scouting Around and Staging

Of course the most business, over 50 percent for food carts and trucks, comes from streetside customers. To find local places to set up, you want to do some reconnaissance prior to setting out with your food truck. Then, once you find a prime location, study the hours when there is enough foot traffic to make it worthwhile. If you find a good location, you may decide to send a "staging car" or two, to park and grab prime real estate while you are loading your truck to drive over. This is your own means of saving a space and keeping competitors at bay in a very competitive business. If parking is legal, you may park your car in the space overnight.

Be careful when breaking into the business. Remember, you are the newcomer on the block. Some of your competitors will be happy to share, especially if your businesses compliment one another, such as a beverage cart and a pizza truck that does not sell beverages. However, many mobile food business owners are very territorial. You don't want to invade someone else's territory. Scott Baitinger of Streetza suggests

When to Re-Apply for a Business License

Even if you are up and running, you may need to re-apply for business licenses if you:

○ Incorporate

○ Add more carts, trucks, trailers, busses, etc.

○ Add catering clients outside of your town or city

○ Change your mode of operation in a major way, such as going from a hot dog cart to a pizza truck.

Check with the various licensing departments to make sure you have the additional licenses when making major changes to your business or to your vehicle. For example, if you upgrade from a smaller truck to a larger (heavier) one, you may need a commercial driver's license.

that you get to know some of your local city council members and store or restaurant owners before selecting your regular location. Neighborhood associations and the local chamber of commerce can also be helpful if you befriend them.

Lending a Helping Hand

In early 2010, many mobile food vehicle owners sent nonperishables and money from their business endeavors to help the people affected by the earthquake in Haiti. Many mobile food vehicle owners have also been front and center during a local crisis or fundraising drive. Providing food during disaster relief or being part of a fundraising drive is a marvelous way to become part of your community. Food carts and trucks have also provided foods to those in need.

In New York City The Woman's Housing and Economic Development Corporation (WHEDco) has been a leader in community development in the South Bronx. Along with being home to four commercial kitchens, the organization is hoping to help utilize food carts in the neighborhood.

"Our green carts project is designed to bring fresh vegetables to areas that otherwise do not usually have such produce readily available," explains WHEDOco President Nancy Biberman, who founded the organization in 1991 after working for many years in an effort to clean up and help rebuild the Bronx. "The green carts is an initiative that was started by the Department of Health in response to concerns about communities that were in need of fresh produce."

While the project is now getting off the ground, it can also help provide jobs to new green cart vendors. "Our goal is also to encourage community members to get involved in this program. We try to advise them on the licensing process and how to become a green cart vendor," adds Kerry McLean, project manager. Hopefully, the project will serve both purposes of providing jobs and bringing fresh produce to areas devoid of such foods.

6

The Work Environment
Commercial Kitchens, Cleaning, and Hiring Help

In all mobile food businesses, you need to be comfortable working on your feet, sometimes for long hours and typically in tight quarters. Standing with a food cart or inside a catering truck in hot weather can get uncomfortable. From a personal hygiene perspective, you'll want to make sure you use deodorant before you start the day and wear sweatbands as needed. Make sure you have a means of keeping yourself cool in the heat of summer. Set up canopies or umbrellas to minimize the heat if you are operating a cart in a sun-drenched area.

As most food business entrepreneurs will tell you, the joy of your job is seeing satisfied customers enjoying your food. Nonetheless, the daily routine can be very tiring with its shopping, food preparation, cleaning, finding your location(s), serving, cleaning some more, returning your vehicle to its home for the night, cleaning some more, and perhaps doing truck repairs. Then there is the business paperwork that needs to get done. Yes, there are a lot of activities that may be part of any given day.

Although you will often be busy whether you are in a kiosk or a bustaurant, you will have slow periods when customers are not lining up. You may want to develop an affinity for reading, although chances are you likely find something that needs to get done. Most mobile food entrepreneurs agree that there is always something to clean or fix or someone to reply to on Twitter.

The Commissary or Commercial Kitchen

Many of you will spend a lot of time in your commercial kitchen. Most jurisdictions require that you have a commercial kitchen if you are cooking food, rather then just heating up food or selling prepackaged foods. The commercial kitchen goes hand in hand with laws preventing you from cooking food at your home or in your vehicle. In the trade, such a commercial kitchen is known as a commissary. Like your vehicle, your commissary kitchen needs to maintain health code standards, which are not unlike those of a restaurant kitchen. These will be spelled out by the local health department. Typically, health inspectors look to make sure food is handled safely and stored properly (at proper temperatures), avoiding problems like salmonella or food poisoning. They also want to make sure that preparation tables and other surfaces can be thoroughly cleaned to prevent bacteria growth. Proper ventilation is also very important. The overall responsibility of making sure the commercial kitchen is up to code is that of the kitchen owners and manager. However, they will pass along their rules to you so that you can help maintain a clean kitchen for all parties concerned.

When renting a commercial kitchen, equipment should typically include:

- A commercial oven
- A large six-burner range. Gas can be cheaper than electric. Convection ovens are popular because of their speed and ability to heat more evenly.
- A microwave oven
- A rotisserie oven

- A flattop grill
- A commercial hood—make sure it was installed by a professional
- A commercial refrigerator— larger is usually better for professional needs
- A walk-in cooler
- A freezer—upright, chest, or walk-in
- A three-part stainless steel sink
- A large dishwasher
- Preparation tables that are durable and easy to clean
- A three-speed mixer with electric lift
- A deep fryer
- Stainless steel cabinets—add as many as you need
- Fire extinguishers—for businesses, not a small residential one
- Rubber floor mats
- Cleaning supplies and rags
- Hand soap and/or sanitizer dispenser
- A mop sink

Renters may need to provide additional supplies and equipment such as those listed below.

- Various pots and pans
- Bowls, plates, and baking sheets
- Utensils
- Ladles, tongs, and spatulas
- Strainers
- Various small appliances

These are just some of the many items found in commercial kitchens. You can bring additional equipment. Inquire about having a place to store whatever you bring so that you do not have to schlep it back and forth with you. In many commercial kitchens, storage areas are provided. If you are cooking on your vehicle, you have to be more selective because all the items listed above are difficult to fit onto most food trucks.

Finding a Commercial Kitchen

You'll want to rent space in a commercial kitchen that is not far from your locations or (ideally) your home. Nonetheless, finding one is not always easy, and building one is

A Typical Commercial Kitchen Ad

Description: Share commercial catering kitchen in Gardena: Day: $350 per 12 hours, monthly: $3,500 minimum. A large 2,500-square-foot catering kitchen includes: 24' hood, 2 Commercial Ovens, 2 Ranges 30" each with 6 burners and oven, 1 Range 30" with broiler and oven, 2 Ranges 30" each with griddle and oven, 2 Deep Fryers, 2 Ranges 15", 1 Convection steamer, 2 Ice makers, Walk-in cooler, 6 Refrigerators 2 and 3 door, 2 Freezers, 6 Stainless steel working tables, 2 Wood working tables, Dish washer, 2 three-compartment dishwashing sinks, 1 two-compartment dishwashing sink, Health department approved—call xxx-xxx-xxxx.

extremely costly. Unless you already own a restaurant, you will most likely be renting your kitchen space. This can be beneficial because you can meet your needs and even share the cost with other renters when ordering supplies.

"I looked online, in the Yellow Pages, and asked people I knew before finding what worked for me. Now, I share a commercial kitchen in an urban part of Seattle," explains Parfait Ice Cream truck owner Adria Shimada. "The space has different stations, so I rent a station and get my own private freezer storage space and the electric hookups I need to run my batch freezer, which is a professional freezer for ice cream."

Two websites that are very helpful when searching for that elusive commercial kitchen are Commercial Kitchen For Rent at commercialkitchenforrent.com, which has a list of commercial kitchens by state, and Culinary Incubator at culinaryincubator.com, which has a map with listings that you can click on.

What You Need to Know about Commercial Kitchens

According to Tom Guiltinan, the CFO and Vice President of WHEDco, the New York–based nonprofit entity that rents three commercial kitchens from one Bronx location, "We try to be accommodating and work with clients to provide the space they need at the times they need." However, it is not always that easy. Guiltinan and other kitchen owners try hard to meet the various needs of clients. "Often businesses who come to us are still growing and aren't completely sure how much kitchen time or space they will need," says Guiltinan, who works with several mobile catering companies.

The WHEDco kitchens are kept in immaculate condition and provide counter space, convection ovens, storage areas, freezers, refrigerators, and most of what any

Inside one of WHEDco's Commercial Kitchens in the Bronx.

client could possibly need, including pots and pans. "Sometimes people share a kitchen and pay less," adds Guiltinan of some of the new business clients. Clients must carry their own liability insurance with a minimum of $2 million for the aggregate coverage and $1 million for incidents. They also need to name WHEDco on the insurance coverage. "Most businesses already have this type of insurance in place," says Guiltinan. He hopes his kitchens, which also provide loading dock access, will soon be a 24/7 operation with a supervisor from the staff on duty at all times to provide security and help in a crisis situation.

Other Options

Schools, churches, temples, as well as local Ys may also have health inspected and certified commercial kitchens available for rent. Discuss your needs and the hours you are looking for. If you find a good match, then draw up a contract. Sometimes restaurants or catering facilities rent out space when they are not being used (which may be late night or early morning). Others have found commercial kitchen space in firehouses and hospitals. The point is—seek and you shall find. And make sure you have your agreement in writing.

Health and Safety First

The importance of kitchen safety cannot be overstated. In your haste to get your menu items out the door and into your kiosk or vehicle, you may find yourselves taking shortcuts. In a word, don't. Accidents and injuries slow you down and can also minimize the quality of your foods.

What Do Customers Want?

Questions you may want to ask when looking for a commercial kitchen include:

○ What are your hours of operations and which hours are available?

○ What is the price? Typically a commercial kitchen will range from $125 to $350 per 10- or 12-hour day. Hourly rates can be anywhere from $10 to $40. Price also depends on the location, kitchen size, and what is included. (Some kitchens do not rent by the hour.) Long-term deals, such as for six months, will usually bring prices down.

○ Are utilities included?

○ Is there an internet WiFi connection?

○ Is all equipment included?

○ How much time can you have at the loading dock and at what hours?

You'll also want to see if the kitchen is clean, includes working (up-to-date) equipment, and has good lighting and good ventilation.

The simplest habit to get into is washing your hands often. Many illnesses are the result of germs traveling from dirty hands. Don't jeopardize your business. You'll also want to make sure all preparation tables, counter tops, and cutting boards are kept clean and that fruits and vegetables are washed in cold water before using.

Other tips for keeping your kitchen (whether on your vehicle or rented) safe from bacteria and accidents include:

1. Storing foods at appropriate temperatures. Make sure to check the temperatures of your refrigerator and freezers often. Cold food should be stored at 38°F or under and hot food at 165°F or above. Between 40° and 140°F is known as the food danger zone. Food should neither be held nor consumed if it is in this temperature range.

Beware!

Whether you are in a commercial kitchen or are allowed to cook in a mobile kitchen, it is very important that you wear clothing that will not get in your way or get caught in machinery. Tuck in shirts, make sure apron strings are tied, and wear comfortable nonslippery shoes with rubber soles, never high heels.

2. Make sure all refrigerator and freezer doors close properly.

3. Keep track of food expiration dates—with a list because you are probably dealing with a lot of foods.

4. Cook foods at a minimum internal temperature and maintain that temperature for at least 15 seconds. This helps kill bacteria.

5. Be particularly careful not to undercook food.

Beware!

It was funny when Monica on the TV sitcom *Friends* lost her earring in the quiche before serving it. It's not so funny when it happens for real. Put all jewelry aside when working in the kitchen or on your vehicle, or simply leave it at home.

6. Adhere to local health codes and go one step beyond. Don't wait for health department inspections to make changes. Do your own inspections. Remember, your reputation is on the line.

7. Check in periodically on the Department of Health website to see if recalls are listed for your area or if there are any new regulations.

8. Check all incoming food shipments carefully. Do not accept anything if it does not appear to be fresh. Also look for damaged cans or boxes.

9. Make sure all food equipment as well as utensils are clean and working properly.

10. Use knives and professional cutlery carefully, which means cutting away from the body and using cutting boards. And if a knife falls, don't try to catch it. Just step back and let it fall—then clean it. Also, never leave knives lying around. Put them away where they belong so nobody working in your kitchen gets injured.

11. Always have potholders and oven mitts handy—and use them. Don't improvise.

12. Have a fire extinguisher handy and make sure you and your employees know how to use it.

13. If you have employees, make sure they know how to properly use all equipment, and if necessary, post instructions.

14. If you are in a commercial kitchen, instructions are typically posted. If not, ask the kitchen manager how something works if you are unsure.

Become Dedicated to Cleaning

You want to have all-purpose cleaners, towels, mops, rags, oven cleaner, cleaning brushes, disinfectants, degreasers, dishwasher detergents, and whatever else is necessary to clean anything you use to prepare or store foods—and kitchen floors, trash receptacles, aprons, etc. Some commercial kitchens provide their own cleaning materials. Use them. You, on the other hand, will be responsible for your vehicle or kiosk.

While dishwashers are nice, they don't always get the job done effectively, so you need to make sure whatever comes out of the dishwasher is cleaned to your liking. If you are in a hurry and need to reuse bowls or other items quickly, you'll need to do your own cleaning with a strong cleaning product followed by air drying—not towels.

Beware!
Ever eat meat that has a fishy taste? Fries that taste a little like asparagus? Apples that smell like Lemon Pledge? Remember to clean your grill, your food slicer, blender, cutting boards, and your preparation utensils when switching from one food to another and make sure no cleaning solution remains.

You also need to make sure tongs and anything else you use to handle food is cleaned regularly. Also clean counters and cutting boards regularly. Don't take short cuts and don't leave things for the proverbial "later." As noted earlier, one of the knocks on mobile food venues has long been that they are not sanitary. All your hard work can and will go down the drain quickly if a customer gets food poisoning or discovers something that should not be in his food. And if a health inspector is not happy, word travels quickly. Remember, social media can sink your business as fast as it can help you grow it. A lot is riding on your dedication to cleanliness.

Establish a Plan

If you establish a plan for cleaning everything and get your employees to follow suit, cleaning can become a simple routine. Brushing off the grill regularly should become a matter of habit that you need not think about. The same goes with wiping down the preparation tables. You will have daily cleaning, such as mopping floors, washing counter tops, and cleaning appliances such as the microwave, coffee maker, can opener, and so on. Floors should actually be cleaned very often with a grease-cutting floor cleaner so that you minimize the chances of anyone falling, including you. You will also have larger jobs that you need not do everyday but still need to do often, such as cleaning the refrigerator(s), ice machines, freezers, and ovens.

Typically the manufacturers of larger appliances have cleaning instructions. Don't throw out the manuals, and write down the websites if you need cleaning tips. Also, don't forget the hood needs to be cleaned a few times a year—by a professional cleaning service. If you are working in a commercial kitchen, this is the owner's responsibility. There will usually be a sticker indicating when the hood was last cleaned.

You'll also want to keep tabs on your cleaning products to make sure you have them all accounted for. Make a list of all cleaning products you need so you can buy them in large quantities when you go shopping or place an order.

Vehicle Presentation

If it isn't enough to spend a significant amount of time cleaning up the kitchen space that you rented (remember, as a renter, you still must clean up your area) and the inside of your vehicle or kiosk, you also need to remember the outside of your vehicle. Nobody wants to buy food from a truck covered with mud (not even from the famous Mud Truck in New York City). Things such as bird poop on the windows won't bring customers flocking to your cart or truck either. Make sure your vehicle is washed and soaped down regularly. Signs should be easily readable and counters should be sparkling. In a bustaurant, the seating area should be as inviting as in the finest restaurant.

FYI

Although your dishwasher is a cleaning machine, it can get dirty, especially with all the wear and tear of steady use. To freshen a dishwasher, while you are cleaning up at the end of your day, try running it empty with some baking soda and vinegar. You should also take out food traps and utensil trays, and clean them as well.

Hiring Help

It's hard to go it alone in any business, especially one that requires you to be chef, server, cleaner, kitchen manager, accountant, driver, and more. While you can run a small cart or truck serving primarily pre-made and/or prepackaged goods on your own, if you should get more elaborate you will probably need some help. Many food truck owners and catering businesses are partnerships or team efforts from the start. Nonetheless, mobile food business owners typically bring on help as they grow or expand. Let's take a look at some of your hiring options.

Hiring a Chef

If you are considering the gourmet route for your business and are not a chef or do not have a particular knack for making some special items, you may want to bring in a chef. Unlike a chef in a restaurant, your menu will most likely be limited. You will, however, want to either discuss the types of food you are looking for or find a chef and see what he brings to the table—or to the plastic or paper plates, as the case may be. In many cases, not unlike a restaurant, the menu is built around the chef. This was the case with the Milford, Connecticut, food truck GoChef, which focused on the cuisine of a top local chef.

Typically, by networking with restaurant owners and others in the culinary field, you can get an idea where to look locally for a chef or a chef's assistant who wants to move up the ranks. You can offer an up-and-comer exposure and the opportunity to create dishes without having to manage the kitchen—you can do that job because many young chefs are primarily interested in using

Smart Tip

Besides having a chef cook for you, it is advantageous to discuss his long-term plans and also let him know what you plan to do to promote your business. Thanks to the Food Network and some well-known food truck owners, media attention is growing for chefs. Let whomever you are thinking about hiring know about your media plans. Don't exaggerate. Be honest!

their culinary skills and not running a kitchen. Of course you need to be ready to compensate a trained chef well, as they are in demand.

One of your prime sources of young talent might be a local culinary school. Another option is to advertise on the internet or look at resumes posted at places like the American Culinary Federation, which links to the American Academy of Chefs at www.acfchefs.org. You can also check out www.ihirechefs.com.

In some cases, you may simply find someone who is a nonprofessional chef but excellent at making a few items. See if she wants to turn her hobby into a career. The Mmmpanadas truck in Texas got started simply because Cody Fields and his wife Kristen, both of whom loved to cook, made damn good empanadas.

Finding Good Help

Yes, another part of your job as a business owner is hiring the help you need. Whether it's a driver, servers for your food, kitchen help, or all of the above, you will need to bring people in to work for you. First, you'll want to know what the going rate is in your part of the country. Typically, you'll find rates in the $8 to $12 an hour category for heating and serving food or helping in the kitchen.

Any person who owns and operates a small business won't hesitate to tell you that one of the most challenging aspects of being a business owner is hiring and retaining good employees. The process of hiring can be daunting if you've never done it before. Most of the labor pool available to help heat up and serve food at your kiosk or in your truck are people looking for temporary jobs while in college or until the latest recession ends. Unless someone is hoping to go into the mobile food or catering business, he or she is unlikely to be with you for years to come.

It is important to keep in mind that the people serving your customers are the frontline representatives of your business. If they are sloppy, rude, or don't do the job right, you can lose customers. With that in mind, you need to look for people who will do a good job. You want people who will:

- Be on time
- Be neat and clean
- Follow the rules and protocol that you have established
- Be courteous to customers
- Give you reasonable notice if they cannot work a shift
- Take the job seriously

Finding Applicants

Word of mouth, posting ads on local job websites and the local Craigslist, or even postings on bulletin boards in your area will generally attract applicants. Keep your postings brief. People are more apt to respond to a few lines than a dissertation. Look for people whom you think might last a while. For example, a college student in her freshman or sophomore year is more likely to stick around longer than a college senior.

If prospective employees are at least 18 (and can prove it) and are interested in a job, take their names and arrange an interview right away. Because you probably do not have a formal office, either meet at your kitchen (if you have one) or pick a neutral location, such as a Starbucks, and sit down to talk. Don't meet people at your home.

Don't Judge a Cook by His Cover

It should go without saying that you want employees who are well groomed. Because employees' appearance is a reflection on the capability of your staff and the quality of your services (and because food is involved), their appearance should be clean-cut, neat, and professional. As for trendy body wear like multiple piercing and tattoos, if you eliminate any young person who expresses him/herself that way, you may not have many candidates to choose from. As long as such personal expressions of individuality do not detract from the person's ability to make and serve food or help you in the kitchen, you should consider them as prospects.

Even though 16-year-olds may work legally in some parts of the country, you may find that some are not as responsible or mature as you would like. Of course it depends on the individual. Employees who are under 18 typically need to have working papers. Ask to see them.

Interviews

Just as job candidates need to prepare before going on job interviews, you also need to be prepared before conducting interviews. To make your life easier, you might print up some basic job application forms, in which

you can ask for basic information, such as name, address, home phone and cell phone numbers, as well as job history and education. You can purchase blank application forms at office supply stores; a package of 100 usually runs about $10. If you create your own forms, keep them simple and straightforward, seeking only relevant information. You can get yourself into trouble by asking personal information, so don't do it.

When interviewing someone, don't fire questions; instead try to create a relaxed atmosphere in which each candidate can explain why she or he would be a good choice for you. Because many young candidates will not have much experience, you are better off asking about their skills and previous experience in general. Then there are the references. They are important, and you should check out all references. You want to get a general idea of the character, reliability, and overall personality of the potential employee. You can also go online and do background checks. Plenty of companies now run such checks for a fee.

In a world where employee theft is a rising concern for most business owners, you have the right to be concerned. Therefore, along with checking references and possibly contacting previous employers, you might want to have a 30- or 60-day trial period as a condition of continuing employment. During that time, you can evaluate a person's natural aptitude for the work, his dependability, and whether he is eating more of your inventory than he is selling.

Job Description

It is also helpful to have a prepared job description that can be given to the candidate. It should include a brief description of the work to be performed, the employee's responsibilities, and the hours. During the interview, explain the job responsibilities and your expectations. Then allow the candidate to do most of the talking. As you listen, watch body language. A confident person will sit up straight in the chair and make direct eye contact with you. Someone who is both articulate and friendly will probably be good with customers. Bilingual candidates may be a plus in certain areas, but don't rule out other good candidates. Someone who looks distracted or has an attitude that indicates that he is only meeting with you because nothing better has come along (yet) may not be your best bet. While it is tough finding work in a bad economy, you cannot let yourself hire out of pity. This is your business. If it goes under because of your employees, you will be feeling a lot more self-pity.

It's possible that you'll make a decision whether to hire someone at the initial interview, but it's better to wait until you've checked references before formally hiring anyone. You should let the applicants know the pay rate so that if it is not enough for the individual, you can cut down on the time and effort it takes to check references.

With all the taxes you are required to pay, it's no wonder some small-business owners pay employees (or themselves) off the books instead of giving Uncle Sam his due. But don't do it. You could find yourself in federal hot water if you're not square with the IRS. Remember, the IRS caught Al Capone and threw Pete Rose and Wesley Snipes in jail. Don't think no one will find out that you're not paying taxes. All it takes is one disgruntled customer, one jealous competitor, or even one angry ex-employee (or ex-spouse) to have your food business go stale.

You're Hired

Hiring someone is always both joyful and nerve-wracking. On one hand, it means you are growing your business, while on the other hand it can mean potential headaches because you are now responsible for someone else. To ease your burden, you need to remember a few simple rules about being the boss.

1. *Listen.* Letting people know what is expected of them is easy. It's also important, however, to listen and hear employee questions, concerns, and occasional good idea.

2. *Be accessible.* Schedule meetings with employees where you can discuss what is going on during the busy workday. Open up a line of communications, and you'll find that you get better results.

Smart Tip

Tip...

Carefully review all safety and health regulations that pertain to your food operation with your employees. You might even walk them through each process and then ask them if they can go through the routine a couple of times. Don't just throw them in a kitchen, behind a cart, or into a truck or bus before you are convinced they know the drill.

3. *Never abuse your power.* Yes, you are the boss and you have the right to expect employees to be alert, responsible, competent, drug-and/or-alcohol free, honest, and diligent about doing their jobs whenever they are on the clock. But you cannot expect nonwork favors nor should you get involved in an employee's home life or personal life.

Rules and Policies

Make sure you have all warnings and proper operating instructions posted and review the correct way of doing everything with employees. Safety is a primary concern to yourself and anyone working for you. For ideas, visit the National Restaurant Association's safety page at: restaurant.org.

Put as much as you can in writing, and make sure your employees see all rules and regulations. Extend this to include policies about missing work and anything else they need to know about the job.

Also, list specific grounds for termination, such as drug or alcohol use on the premises, arriving at work under the influence of drugs or alcohol, stealing, carrying an unlicensed weapon onto the property, or any lewd, rude, or violent behavior to a customer or another employee. Also include a sexual harassment policy that spells out how such matters will be handled—typically by using an impartial arbitrator. False harassment claims can be as damaging as real ones.

You want to be covered in case an employee or former employee decides to sue you. In a litigious society, lawsuits are common and can seriously jeopardize your business. Have all employees read your policy statement or handbook and sign that they have read it. Keep the signed paper in a safe place. This gives you written proof that they have been informed of what is expected of them.

Smart Tip

Tip...

Be fire safe. To prevent fires, store towels, food packaging, oils, pressurized containers, and other combustibles away from stovetops and ovens. Keep exhaust fans and ductwork free of grease build-up and regularly inspect and test fire suppression systems.

Taxes

No discussion of business, or hiring employees, would be complete without bringing up your obligations to good old Uncle Sam. As an employer, you will be required to withhold several different types of taxes from your employees, including income tax, FICA (aka Social Security), and Medicare. The IRS also requires you

Tip...

Smart Tip

Keep your employees involved in the business. Ask their opinions of menu items, listen to their ideas regarding ways to move customers along faster, and so on. Some degree of involvement in the business makes for much better employee morale. And if someone makes a mistake, you should simply explain how it needs to be done. Do not criticize or ridicule the employee. They will not want to work for you, and it will show in their lack of productivity. Unhappy employees can reflect upon your business.

to keep detailed records about the amount withheld and when it was sent in to the IRS. You will be expected to pay on schedule.

You should have an accountant for your business who will set you up with a system for paying federal, state, and local taxes in a timely fashion and recording these tax payments properly. For more information about withholding and taxes, pick up a copy of IRS Publication 15-B, *Employer's Tax Guide*, as well as Publication 583, *Starting a Business and Keeping Records*. You can find both on the IRS website at irs.gov or at your local IRS office.

FICA

Employers incur a tax liability for every employee. You must pay the matching portion of the FICA tax, which, as of 2010, is 6.2 percent, and the matching portion of Medicare taxes, which as of 2010 is 1.45 percent. Also, workers' compensation insurance payments are mandatory in all states except Texas. They cover employees' medical expenses and disability benefits if they're injured on the job. The amount varies by state, so contact your state labor department for guidance on how much to set aside.

Smart Tip

Lucky you—the federal government has made paying your business taxes easier with EFTPS-Direct. This free electronic payment method allows you to pay by PC or phone using your employer identification number or Social Security number. You'll also need to provide bank routing information so your account can be debited. For more information or to enroll, call (800) 945-8400, or log on to eftps.gov.

If You Park It, They Will Come—or Not

Marketing and Promotion

Good food and service with a smile are important, but if nobody knows you are serving, you're out of luck. Marketing and promotion are key factors in the success of almost any business. While you don't necessarily need a full marketing plan, early on in your overall planning process you want to think about how you will attract customers.

What's In a Name?

One of the first steps is to choose a good name, one that will draw attention. Many cart vendors, especially in Manhattan, have long been known simply by their location. People will comment on the great hot dogs from the guy on 57th Street and Fifth Avenue or 23rd and Park, but with so much competition today, it is advantageous to have a memorable name for your business.

There are plenty of clever names on the sides of food trucks, trailers, carts, and busses. Some business owners, such as Scott Baitinger and Steve Mai of Streetza pizza, had the fans name the truck, which enhanced their fan connection. Others held local contests. Some are extensions of established businesses, typically a restaurant. Still others came from websites like crowdsourcing.com, where people submitted names and the person with the best name gets paid for her idea. Most, however were the result of some brainstorming with family and clever friends. Sometimes, you'll get an idea from someone you least expected. On the television sitcom Rosanne, in the pre-food truck craze, when the Conners were opening a small diner from which to serve lunch, Dan and Roseanne asked their 9-year-old son D.J. what name he would use. He replied "The Lunch Box," and lo and behold it stuck and became the name of their business. So, ask around.

Some truck owners draw attention with word plays like the Taste No Evil Muffins truck in Austin. You could always try a twist on a known name, such as the India Jones

---

Know Your Foods

Can you guess what each of these food trucks, or carts sell?

1. Let's Be Frank in Los Angeles and San Francisco
2. The Paddy Wagon in Los Angeles
3. The Dump Truck in Portland, Oregon
4. Yellow Submarine in Miami
5. Man Bites Dog in Austin

Yep, these are all real food trucks.

If you answered 1. Franks, 2. Burgers, 3. Dumplings 4. Submarine Sandwiches and 5. Hot dogs, you're correct.

Chow Truck in Los Angeles, Chairman Bao in San Francisco, or Jack and the Bean Bowl in Boston.

Typically, you want your name to express what you sell in a clever manner. The Cupcake Truck in New Haven or the Cupcake Stop in New York City may not be as clever, but they get the point across and generate a lot of business. The Big Gay Ice Cream Truck in New York City also gets its point across while Big Ass Sandwiches in Portland gets the point across with emphasis!

The point is, let your foods and/or ethnic menu and your location lead the way. Consider the following names to get your creative juices going:

- Only Burgers in Durham (NC)
- The Sausage Guy in Boston
- Schnitzel and Things in New York City
- La Dominique Crepes in Philadelphia
- Cookie WagSF in San Francisco
- Whiffies Deep-Fried Pie Cart in Portland (OR)
- Cuties Pie Wagon in Austin (TX)
- Kooper's Chowhound Burger Wagon in Baltimore

Or consider the following ethnic names:

- The Texas Cuban in Austin (TX)
- Japa Dog in Vancouver (Japanese-style hot dogs)
- Tamale Tracker in Chicago
- Fish Lips Sushi Truck in Los Angeles

You can always simply include the meal you serve, such as the Brunch Box in Portland or the Dessert Truck in New York. You can also include your vehicle in the name, like the Magic Curry Kart in San Francisco or the Icycle Bicycle in Los Angeles. Of course rhyming a food with the word "kiosk" is virtually impossible. In fact, it is actually listed as one of a few words in the English language with which nothing rhymes.

Searching for Business Names

Make sure to do a business name search before registering. You do this for three reasons:

1. It ensures that no one else in your local area is using the name

2. It makes your local authorities happy. This way, they can keep tabs on you for tax or other licensing purposes, and you go on public record in case anyone needs to look up the name of your company and find the name of the owner.

3. Most banks won't allow you to open a business checking account unless you can show them that you have registered your business name.

> **Tip...**
>
> ### Smart Tip
> Keep names short and easy to remember, especially for those looking for you on a social media platform. Also, avoid generic names like Fred's Food Truck. Unless Fred is famous, it doesn't stand out or tell you what foods are featured.

See if your county clerk's office already has your chosen name on the books. Have a few variations ready in case one or two names are already taken. If your name is specific to your product, your own name, or the name of your city, such as Boston Bob's Bacon and Beans, the less likely someone else has claimed it. Typically, whether a business owner has a website or not, the company name will come up if you do a Google search, so you might try that before doing an official search at the county clerk's office. You can also contact the local chamber of commerce or simply look in the local Yellow Pages. If a name has a trademark, you can search the United States Patent and Trademark Office at uspto.gov or 1-800-786-9199 (toll free). You can also check the Thomas Register (thomasnet.com) for registered and unregistered trademark names. It's a cross-industry database that includes hundreds of thousands of trademarks and service marks. Network Solutions is another place to look for business names online (networksolutions.com).

Registering Your Business Name

You can register your business name locally and also obtain a trademark if you choose to register your brand. First, you will do a trademark search by going to the free trademark database on the USPTO's website. Go to the USPTO's Trademark Electronic Business Center (uspto.gov) and choose "search" under the trademark section. Then follow the instructions on the screen. You'll also get all the information on how to obtain a U.S. trademark or service mark. It's not necessary for a small local business, but as your business grows, you might want to expand and sell your brand (your foods) in retail outlets. Get more information at the U.S. Trademark and Patent Office at uspto.gov.

Vehicle Design

The Dim and Dem Sum truck in Cleveland is considered to have one of the more noteworthy food truck designs with a bright red octopus over bright yellow and orange stripes. Keeping an Asian-inspired theme, the truck was designed by an anonymous graffiti artist in Cleveland.

The Los Angeles skyline on the side of the bright yellow Palace food truck and the Philadelphia skyline aboard the Sugar Truck are both inspiring and eye catching. You also want to be attention grabbing like the bright red Mmmpanadas truck in Austin, Texas. Bright colors, bold lettering, and/or artwork are part of the latest in popular mobile food vehicles. Think big, bold, and exciting.

The Concept

The Louisiana Territory truck in San Jose is built around the concept of serving Louisiana-style foods, including Shrimp and Sausage Creole over rice and Louisiana Smoked Sausage. The Grilled Cheese truck in LA is big and yellow, with a yellow menu featuring the signature Cheesy Mac and Rib and an online gallery of cheesy photos. Meanwhile, Van Leeuwen Artisan Ice Cream in New York City is designed to be an old-fashioned ice cream parlor on wheels with freshly made ice cream and classic sundaes.

The days of the basic food cart or truck have given way to a new brand of vehicles with concepts, or themes, that carry through from exterior design to logos, menus, and of course the foods. Your concept should be a means of distinguishing you from your competition and building your niche market. You might even name some of your foods in line with your theme, such as the Yellow Submarine in Miami which also sells the Lady Madonna sandwich, named from another Beatles song, or the Big Gay Ice Cream Truck in New York, which serves the Bea Arthur. Be clever and consistent (never confusing), and you can broaden your appeal and even draw media attention.

Vehicle Wraps

You can opt for a specially designed vinyl wrap that fits around your mobile business or kiosk. Food vehicle wraps are a marvelous and cost-effective means of advertising because they look professional and are on your vehicle 24/7, generating the attention of potential customers. Advertising Vehicles (advertisingvehicles.com) is one of a number of businesses in the vehicle wrap business. Cliff Digital (cliffdigital. com) is one of many design companies that now has a section for vehicle wraps on its website as does San Diego vehicle wraps (sandiegovehiclewraps.com). You can find many more companies online.

Food cart and truck designers are enjoying the growth of the business while turning out some first-rate designs. Vehicle or kiosk designers are typically found on the web or

Branding

Consider your brand or the character of your vehicle or kiosk. That means having a consistent theme from the look of the truck to the napkins, menu, and other accessories to the way you present the food. You can be pink and playful, dark and mysterious, ethnic, silly, or whatever suits your fancy—but go with the theme. The Fojol Brothers of Merlindia created an entire world of their own that has generated a lot of media attention with their food truck in Washington, DC—their website at fojols.com is unique and entertaining. Foodies today are into the overall ambiance and brand of their favorite mobile food vendors.

through word of mouth. Food Cart USA (foodcartusa.com), All Star Carts and Kiosks (www.allstarcarts.com), and Cart King (cart-king.com) design first-rate mobile food vehicles both inside and out. They also walk you through other steps, such as making sure their interior design will meet your local health and safety codes. Road Stoves (Roadstoves.com) not only customizes the interiors and exteriors of food trucks, but also provide commissary parking in the Los Angeles area plus truck maintenance and security.

Your Logo

A logo can set your vehicle apart from the competition. It is a distinguishing graphic representation of your business and its value. You can use the trademark symbol TM to indicate that it is your logo, even if it is not yet an official trademark.

Look for local designers and artists to come up with logos and graphics for your business. Sometimes you'll find great talent just waiting to be discovered in local art classes or art schools. Ask around. Because your truck will be unique onto itself, other cart or truck owners may recommend artists or designers. Save yourself and the artist or designer some time by looking at some of his previous works before asking him to do something for you.

Menu Design

Design your menu to fit the style and theme of your truck. Selling cupcakes? Post the menu on the cart in the shape of a cupcake. You'll want a menu that is appropriate with your brand and style, so use your color scheme and design. Read as many menus as you can find from your competitors. Get an idea of what styles and layouts you like.

Some menus simply list the offerings with prices while others include some detail about the menu items. For example Adria in the Parfait Ice Cream truck describes her flavors:

Butter Toffee Crunch

We make our own butter toffee, coated with dark chocolate and hazelnuts, and then add generous chunks of this delicious confection to our vanilla bean ice cream. The result is a better tasting version of "Heath Bar Crunch" without any of the artificial or hydrogenated ingredients in industrially manufactured candy.

Such descriptions can enhance your brand by letting customers know that your foods are all-natural or from a interesting locations. Have various versions of menus for various locations—for example, your website menu can include more detail than the small posted menu or a sandwich board. Consider where your menus will be posted, such as on your:

FYI

For comprehensive up-to-date information about truck designs, marketing, menus, health codes, or practically anything else going on in the mobile food truck industry, check out Mobile Food News (mobile food news.com).

- Vehicle
- Website
- Printed materials
- Sandwich boards (perhaps)

Design accordingly so that your foods and prices are easily readable for those in a hurry.

Social Media

Twitter, FourSquare, and Facebook have become the latest marketing tools for mobile food entrepreneurs to stay in touch with their customers and fans. "New technology has been a big game changer, allowing trucks to pick up and move to where customers are on short notice," wrote Katy McLaughlin on SmallBiz.com. in her January 2010 article "Food Truck Nation."

Scott Baitinger of Streetza explains that he and his partner use Twitter to let people know their location and also to tell stories about customers, show photos of them, and build a community. Dennis Quint of the Big Gay Ice Cream Truck is selective about answering tweets because there are so many, but he does want to maintain a dialogue with his customer base so that they enjoy a connection to their favorite truck.

Twitter

The free social networking and microblogging site has become a favorite of mobile food vendors. You can get started by going to Twitter.com and setting up an account. You should use your business name while creating an account. Then, by clicking on Join the Conversation, you can begin sending tweets, which are 140 character messages, or updates. You can also read those of others. The best part about Twitter is that it is an interactive media tool that keeps you updated in the moment.

"If you are going to open up this type of two-way conversation, you shouldn't just use it for one-way communication. Twitter is all about engaging your followers. You can't respond to every tweet, but if you are going to show that you care about your followers, you should write back often," explains social media expert and consultant Kris Ruby, president of Ruby Media Group LLC in Westchester, New York.

Facebook

You can sign up on Facebook.com for a free account by clicking on "Sign Up." A form will appear, and you need to fill it out as a business. Then, following some standard security checkpoints, you will get a confirmation e-mail from the folks at Facebook and you will be all set. You'll then want to set up a profile of your business complete with photos of your food and your vehicle.

"Give people a reason to respond. Ask open-ended questions, make a game out of it," says Kris Ruby, adding it's important to bring people into your marketing. "Facebook pages have worked very well for businesses." And, she adds, updating your page often is important.

Phone Applications

There is a growing market of applications you can buy for the latest mobile phones, including those that provide users with the nearest restaurants or the location of the nearest food trucks or carts. Many of these applications are for the iPhone, while others, such as the popular Foursquare, will work on a Blackberry as well as on other smart phones.

Foursquare is all about letting your fans know where you are at any given time. It also allows for customers to do shout outs, which could be a comment about their favorite foods, such as "I love the Guacamole Burger!" The person with the most shout outs (for that day) becomes the mayor.

> **FYI**
>
> Los Angeles has been a forerunner in the food truck revolution. The iPhone application "LA Street Food" has become popular in the area. Look for similar apps for other major cities.

"It's a good marketing idea to reward the mayor with a free burger, taco, ice cream cone, or whatever you sell," adds Kris Ruby, who stresses the importance of not just letting people know where you are but also building a steady following.

Other restaurant locating applications are quickly adding the mobile food industry to their listings. Food Truck, a $.99 iPhone application, now tracks trucks in eight major cities including New York and Los Angeles.

Your Website

A website is essential, even if you are using Facebook, Twitter, and various mobile applications. Plain and simple, people still use the web to find out about a business. Your website is another tool in your marketing plan.

Designing Your Website

A new business owner should look at the sites of similar businesses to get an idea of the look that he wants for the website. While you cannot take someone else's content, you can get the general idea of the layout and even the colors you want.

Typically your website will contain the following:

- *Homepage*. Photos of the food, photos of the truck, easy links to the other pages on your site (such as your About Us pages), your Twitter thread, and the most relevant current news is typically found on the homepage. Like the rest of the site, the homepage should take on the colors and concept of your vehicle or kiosk. You should also include a link to your Facebook page and anywhere else you can be located. You might have your menu on the homepage; if not, it should be a click away,

- *About Us*. Tell your story in a brief and clever way. Read other About Us pages to get an idea of what to say and then in your own words tell the story of how you got started and why. People don't need your life story so edit, edit, edit.

- *Menu*. Display your menu on a colorful, eye-catching page in conjunction with your colors. Make sure to update foods and prices as they change.

- *Gallery*. Some recent pictures of the foods, the truck, customers (with their

Smart Tip

Don't forget your website is up there day after day. Update it often. Keep it current. Provide some content. Be informative and entertaining. Give people a reason to keep coming back.

Tip...

signed consent), and even you as the owner(s) can be posted. Update if you attended a recent event or have something new to show.

- *Press.* Newspapers and magazines are clamoring to write about the latest in mobile foods—as soon as you get coverage, post it on your website.

- *Map and/or Schedule.* If you know where you're going to be in the next week or next month, post a schedule and/or map.

- *Contact Page.* Make sure people can reach you easily.

Smart Tip

Link to other sites and have them link to you. The Mmmpanadas website (mmm panadas.com), for example, links to some of the best places to find fresh food in the Austin area and places where they shop. These sites then provide reciprocal links.

For a catering company handling parties and other outings, you'll want to have a little more detail on your website because clients can hire you or at least inquire directly about such services from your site.

Your website should immediately convey what you can offer clients and why you should be their choice to hire. This can be done through photos of parties and celebrations you have catered, along with photos of food and even a few themes. (Get permission from clients to use photos from their events.) Also on your site should be your business name and logo, easily accessible contact information, and details on what kinds of catering you do with sample themes and menus. You may want to include a few short testimonials. Keep them brief because nobody wants to read an endless review. Also, try to maximize your responses by offering online deals, such as 10 percent off if you respond via e-mail. Your goal is to start a dialogue about what catering needs a client may have and how you can fulfill them.

Once people respond to your website, make a smooth and early transition from e-mails to a phone call and even an in-person meeting to show them what you can do for them. Of course, you also need to make it clear, on the website, exactly where you do business. If you're based in Ann Arbor, Michigan, for example, someone from Boise, Idaho, probably won't be in your catering area. Don't quote prices on your website, although you can give a range. Typically you'll use a per person rate on a tiered level, with more expensive items, such as prime filet mignon at one level and chicken at another for a dinner. Also provide options and offer lower prices for more people, such as 50 people bringing a menu choice from $25 per person to $22 per person. More on pricing later.

Web Layout and Design

It's important to put the most important data and great photos high up on the pages so that people need not scroll down and down. You can keep older information farther down, such as an event you attended a month ago, but keep recent and important news up high on the page(s). Also make sure your colors and graphics look good not only on your computer screen but also on various mobile devices because more and more people are using their BlackBerrys, Droids, and phones as their computers. Don't waste time on fancy graphics that may take too long to load. Nobody has time to wait.

If you look for a local web designer in your area, make sure to show her other sites that you like, and be sure that she develops a site that is user-friendly and easy to maneuver. It's your business, so get what you want. For your purposes, the site does not need to have sales capabilities unless you are selling promotional items like T-shirts.

From a technical standpoint, it is important that all pages link easily to the information the individual is seeking. Don't make visitors to your website jump hurdles to find what they are looking for or they will give up. Check links often to make sure they are still working. Note: Many websites today are built on GoDaddy (godaddy.com), which makes it easy to put together a site.

One great example of a food truck website comes from the Nom Nom Truck (nomnomtruck.com). The website captures the concept and the culture behind the truck as well as the foods and the owners, Misa and Jen, in a very uplifting and colorful manner. It even explains what a Banh Mi, a menu favorite, is made of. Among the other excellent websites to check out are parfaiticecream.com, themudtruck.com (although you don't need such elaborate opening graphics, the site is a testimony to the brand and their conviction), and samschowdermobile.com.

Establishing an Online Presence

As many business owners have learned over the past decade, just because you have a website doesn't mean people will find it. Even if you optimize your site with key words, links, and other tricks of the trade, that still doesn't assure you that people will flock to it.

You need to maintain a presence on Twitter and have your website and Facebook page clearly printed on your menus and in any media interviews you do. Linking with others also draws attention to your website. Good content about food and topics your audience can munch on is also important in building a following and increasing hits.

Blogging is very popular these days, but you need to make your blog is interesting and fun to read. Also, drawing in new business by adding tidbits of clever information, trivia, e-cards, jokes, or anything else relating to your food or your overall theme is beneficial. Then add a "Forward to a Friend" tab to start viral marketing. People like to send short, clever tidbits to their buddies. This way your followers can help promote your business.

Marketing and Promotional Ideas

Once upon a time a food truck or food cart might have been located nearby a new store in hopes of trying to capture the crowd as they left the grand opening. Today, a food truck is often a co-star, or in some cases a main attraction. Ever since the "Great Food Truck Race" aired on the *Food Network* in August 2010, many trucks and carts have taken on personalities of their own. Yet it takes some work to continue building a following, especially as more competition hits the streets.

Giveaways

One of the most tried and true means of building a following is by giving something away, whether it's a promotional item or a sample of your product, which in this case means food. Providing it fits into your marketing budget, consider giveaways as a standard means of generating a crowd. Food companies have been doing this for years by providing free samples in supermarkets.

Contests

You can promote a simple contest through social media as well as from your vehicle. You might, for example, look for someone to name your latest culinary extravaganza (aka your latest food creation). Prizes need not be spectacular, just enough to convince fans to participate. Make a big deal about the drawing of the winner so that people will be on hand and buying your food!

Word-of-Mouth Marketing

Just give 'em something to talk about. The cheapest means of spreading the word is by having others do it for you, which is also a form of viral marketing. There are many ways in which you can set up a "Tell a Friend" 15 percent discount. You could also pull a stunt of sorts, much like Starbucks did by attaching cups to the roofs of cars. The cars then drove around and anyone who flagged the driver to let her know her coffee cup was on the roof of the car received a free cup of coffee. No, you don't have the budget of Starbucks, but on a smaller scale you can do something simple, legal, and attention grabbing in your area. Singing and dancing servers might get you noticed, or perhaps you can have someone dressed up as a mascot to hand out balloons and coupons near your location.

Attending or Staging Local Events

Find out about local events in advance. If you believe the turnout will make it worth your while, plan to attend, which usually means reserving a space. You can also do what some food truck owners have done and stage a party or something like a puppet show for kids if you sell ice cream. Be creative.

Advertising and Sponsorships

Food magazine advertises on a food truck. Why not? It generates attention for the magazine and income for the food truck owners. Yes, you can sell advertising or trade with other businesses. Put their ads on your menu and your ad in their storefront or on their menu. Bartering for ad space is a great deal because you have mobile visibility and/or distribution. It's also a plus because paying for advertising can become costly very quickly.

From a sponsorship standpoint, you can be a sponsor of a local event such as a local race for a local charity. This shows your business off while you help a worthy cause. A business running an event could also bring you in as an added attraction. For example, ABC Family, while launching its summer TV lineup, hired a food truck to give out free cupcakes. This brought the food truck to the attention of a new audience of cupcake lovers.

Let other business owners know that you can be bought or even be asked to show up if it looks like there will be a good turnout. Look to become a part of your community. Sponsor a youth sports team or turn up at a blood drive. The more visibility you have locally, the more you build your reputation.

Customer Relations: Service with a Smile

One of the simplest ways of drawing repeat customers doesn't involve technology nor does it require you to dip into your budget. It is simply by having good customer relation skills. This begins with a smile, a polite thank-you, and paying attention to the needs of your customers. Courtesy has become a dying art. Don't let your truck be part of this demise. Train your employees to be accommodating, polite, and courteous at all times. If there is a problem, make sure they are ready and willing to do what is necessary to solve it to the customer's satisfaction. Remember, your reputation is on the line, and with the immediacy of social media, the last thing you need is someone badmouthing your business.

Public Relations

No, you don't want to spend thousands of dollars a month on a public relations firm when you can spread the word yourself through social media and by word of mouth. You do, however, want to get into the mass media if at all possible. Generating stories about your business, whether in a blog or a televised news report, can draw customers and will cost you next to nothing.

Because more and more writers and reporters are now covering the mobile food industry and food trucks and/or carts have been featured in all sorts of major publications, it's not all that hard to get coverage. In fact, many food truck websites now feature a page of press clippings.

From a kiosk to a bustaurant, you can generate attention through:

- New and innovative menu items
- The concept and design of your kiosk or vehicle
- Special promotional activities or events
- Partnering with a major store or well-known business
- Expanding with additional vehicles or kiosks
- Hiring a chef with a following

Of course good food and good service is a big plus when trying to generate media attention.

> **Tip...**
>
> **Smart Tip**
> Get a feel for which web-sites your demographic visits and which magazines or local newspapers they read. Get the name of the editor and/or web content manager, and tweet or e-mail that person. It's very important to reach the right individual. Also, take note of writers and reporters who have written about mobile food previously and save their information. Don't send them every little bit of information. Wait until you have something interesting, enticing, or mouth watering to report.

For your part, you need to contact any and all local publications as well as websites that follow the mobile food industry or write about the latest trends. You can tweet a local reporter or blogger, or for longer news items, e-mail a one-page press release. Make sure to keep your information concise, stick to the point, and lead with the most exciting and eye-catching aspect of your news. Focus on news that might be of interest to your following. You can hire a local freelance PR writer for help or look online for press release writing tips.

If a reporter, blogger, or publisher wants to write about you or cover you on television or on a website, be easily accessible with contact info at the ready. Don't put off interviews—the media moves quickly and news today may not be of interest tomorrow.

Mobile Event Catering

While mobile catering is sometimes used to sum up all types of mobile food vehicles, in this book mobile catering is defined as those businesses that cater specific events in various places. Much of what has been discussed thus far—such as menu options, licenses, hiring employees, startup costs, and finding a commercial kitchen—apply to mobile catering trucks. However, there are some key differences that are discussed in this chapter.

Catering Business Fundamentals

To run an effective catering business, you need to start by figuring out what type of catering best suits you. It's hard to be everything to every potential client, especially when starting out. As your business grows, you can take on more challenges, larger parties, and more adventurous themes. To begin, however, you should start with some manageable ideas. Perhaps you have a few themes that you do well that would be great for cocktail parties or kids parties.

You can offer to cater events much in the manner that a food truck works a festival, by parking and serving—only in your case you are strictly for hire and not selling individual items. If permitted in your jurisdiction, you can cook on your vehicle. Most mobile caterers, however, use a commercial kitchen and transport food to parties and/or local events. Unlike a food truck or cart making a daily run, however, you may not have a set schedule when starting out. You will probably have occasional bookings—three one week and perhaps none the next—so you need to discuss flexible scheduling with the kitchen representative. Unfortunately, using a commercial kitchen on such a scattered basis typically costs you a more than having a set long-term deal. Look for a kitchen that can provide such flexibility and work with you as you grow.

Know Your Market

Before you can cater to a niche market, you need to know what is popular at such occasions. What foods are being served at:

- Nonprofit groups and associations
- Corporate lunches and parties
- Kids parties
- Special celebrations/parties (graduations, retirement parties, Bar/Bat Mitzvahs)
- Charitable events
- Red-carpet opening nights
- Engagement parties and weddings

While you may not be the next Tareq and Michaele Salahi (the infamous White House party crashers), you can still scout all sorts of gatherings. If you can't finagle an invitation, then ask people you know to take notes on each of the catered events they attend. Scout your competition to see what they've cooked up. Take note of whether any parties have made the local food pages, gossip columns, or websites. Play detective, and figure out menu options for each of the demographic groups. Remember, you can't please every group—yet. Keep in mind that weddings are probably the most challenging events to cater because so much is riding on them and you need to have a very solid reputation.

Corporate events and kids' parties will obviously want different menu items. But what does the red-carpet crowd eat in your area? What are popular snacks for retirement parties? What does the late night chic crowd eat? Again, know what you can make and make well. Then determine which groups are best for you to approach.

Setting Up Your Menu

Of course you need to decide on your menu items. They will be built around what you (or your chef) know how to make, the size of the parties you feel comfortable catering, and the types of parties you are planning to cater.

After researching your potential market, you need to consider what menu best suits your needs. Remember to factor in the availability of foods in your area, how much help you will have preparing food, and the time element from booking a client to the actual event. It's advantageous to set a deadline for changes, such as three days in advance or even a week for larger parties. After that clients cannot change menu items or the number of guests without an additional fee. The more you can plan a h e a d, the better off you will be. To play it safe, you can have some last-minute options always at the ready, such as pastas, salads, and other items that won't cost you much to have on hand.

Your menu is also predicated on the cost of foods. The more you spend, the more you need to charge. With that in mind, you should look at a markup of three times your expenses. So if a specific dish costs you $7 to buy and prepare per serving, you would need to charge $21 per person for that menu item. Have a variety of menu choices at different price points. People like variety. Lunches can be hot or cold, pastas, meats, fish, salads, sandwiches, quiche, etc., while the main

FYI

The USDA has a standard for nutritious eating. It follows what is called the Food Pyramid. This pyramid consists of recommended percentages of grains, vegetables, fruits, dairy products, and meat and beans for a healthy diet. When making up your menu, consider these five important categories, especially in a health-conscious environment.

Catering Themes

Start with one or two themes and plan menus accordingly. Later on you can always expand the list if business is going well. Popular themes include:

- ○ Comfort foods
- ○ Outdoor BBQs
- ○ Clam bakes or picnics for groups or associations
- ○ Ethnic dining (Mexican fiesta, A Taste of Italy, New Orleans, etc.)

course for a dinner is typically a choice of fish, poultry, or meat, plus a vegetarian offering. Of course this can vary depending on your theme or demographic group. For kids' parties, you might opt to go with hot dogs, chicken fingers, or fish sticks, which is a variation on meat, chicken, or fish, plus pasta as a vegetarian choice. Also offer various ways of preparing dishes, such as grilled, roasted, poached, or fried. And remember to cater to people with various food preferences, such as vegan or kosher, as well as those individuals with food allergies. Be prepared. Try to avoid offering to customize a menu for a client. It's better to stick with what you know than promising them anything. Trying something new may be cost ineffective, and even worse, it may not turn out very well unless someone on your staff knows how to make it.

Marketing Ideas

Because you have no brick-and-mortar storefront and are not driving around unless you are headed to/from an event, you need to do more marketing than restaurants or mobile food vendors.

You want to get your name to as many event planners as possible, and if you go the wedding route, you'll want to become known to wedding planners as well. Some marketing ideas include:

- Using the social network to talk about your themes and your menu choices
- Starting a blog on recipes and food
- Spreading the word among friend, family members, and neighbors, as well as local organizations and associations

- Making sure to have business cards to hand out everywhere
- Having a brochure with photos of your foods and a list of themes included—and hand them out often
- Building your website and maintaining it with interesting content

Unlike the mobile food trucks and carts, your location is not important on your website. Instead you want to feature your upcoming availability, your menu, and your themes. Of course you also need to make sure clients know how they can reach you. It is also a good idea to promote upcoming themes in advance. For example, start hyping your seasonal holiday party themes at least six months ahead of time. Note: It can be advantageous to check out the website of the National Association of Catering Executives (nace.net).

Smart Tip

Along with developing several menu options (not too many) for your catering business, you should also think about seasonal favorites so that you can be ready to do the corporate Fourth of July summer barbeque as well as the corporate holiday party. Remember, return business is very important. Plan your clients' next party even before they think of it, and let them know you are ready when they are. You might even send them a tasty treat with a reminder that the holidays are coming up and holiday parties are one of your specialties.

Of course the most important way of getting started is by serving great food at a party or luncheon and making sure people talk about it. The best way to do this is to offer your services at a few small parties or luncheons at an unbeatable price—free. Yes, this will be part of your startup cost, but if you get a few jobs under your belt and generate some buzz, word of mouth can have you making back your investment in a hurry. Catering is very much a word-of-mouth business. If someone likes what you serve and how you manage the party, they will tell their friends. Also, get some positive testimonials and put them on your website.

Beware!

Never book a party or event until you know exactly how much you can prepare and store in your kitchen and carry on your vehicle.

Professionalism

You need to be as professional as possible when working parties. This is especially important for your staff. Matching attire is in vogue, although you may not need uniforms or black tie (unless your specialty is black tie affairs such as weddings). As least have shirts or vests with your logo on them for a professional look—and to promote your business.

Learning to Serve

Your staff may also need a crash course on serving etiquette. There are proper ways to serve and to act when catering a party. "Teaching people how to serve and act while catering a party is one of the topics we teach under Dining Etiquette," says Laura Katen of Katen Consulting (katenconsulting.com) in Westchester, New York. A well-trained staff can enhance your chances of being hired for upcoming gatherings.

You need to discuss the details of an upcoming party or event with your clients, spelling out exactly what you can offer. Know your capabilities. Sure you might have a maximum of 50 for an office party, but can you cook for 20 more and price accordingly? Flexibility is very important, as is knowing what is beyond your limits.

It's important that you are as professional as possible when meeting with prospective clients. Because you are a mobile business, you should either visit a client's office (with something tasty) or meet at a neutral location (again with something tasty—but if you meet in a Starbucks or a restaurant, minimize the goodies).

Catering Contracts

It is professional to have a contract in place for any event you are catering. Sit down with an attorney (one who is good with contracts) and spell out all the possible scenarios. Have clients sign contracts that include the where and when of the event, the foods they have selected, the quantity, and the costs. Also make sure you have a very specific arrangement when it comes to payment. A deposit is common. Also make it clear that the bill is due at the end of the event or when you deliver the food if you are not being hired to serve. Let them know acceptable means of payment. Also don't forget to attend to the what-ifs in your contract. What if it is an outside party and there is inclement weather? Do you offer a partial refund? Can you handle the move to an indoor location? Do you charge more for setting up twice? How much? What if you are catering a party for adults, but there are five young children, do you charge them less per person? Do you charge them at all? Do you have kid-friendly foods available? You should, at a lower price. Consider all of the possibilities.

From Setup to Cleanup

If you will be serving at a party, visit the location in advance (or at least get an overview of the room) before you arrive with food and any decorations. You'll want to come in ready to set up with a clear idea of the facility. If you need to supply tables and chairs, know that in advance and be ready to set up. Many catering companies do not take on that extra burden because it means a larger truck or even a separate truck.

Smart Tip

If you are starting out small, part time, on weekends, or simply just getting your feet wet, you might only need expensive equipment and supplies a couple of days a week. In such a case, you might consider leasing some of your equipment.

Make sure to map out everything from setup to cleanup and know who will handle each task, especially getting rid of debris. When you leave a location, it should look exactly as it did before you arrived. If you need electrical outlets, find out where they are. Have a small, quiet portable generator just in case. Know what you need and what they require in advance so you can be as inconspicuous as possible.

Food Transport

There are a lot of tricks to the trade, many of which you will learn as you go forward. In fact, most caterers have developed their own systems over time. One of the most important things to remember is that food must be ready to go at the time specified in your agreement. With this in mind, you'll want to get cold dishes, especially those that need to be cooked, out of the way and into the refrigerator in advance, so they have time to cool down before the trip. The bottom line is that some foods are better choices for catering because they travel well. Chilled or room-temperature dishes such as salads, soups, and braised foods work well, while foods that can dry out can be a problem. Know ahead of time which foods travel better than others and what you can do to keep foods fresh and moist when serving.

Beware!

Something smells fishy. If hot foods will be out on the buffet for a period of time, some may start to smell. Fish is especially delicate. Opt for crab cakes or fried oysters, or sell clients on your delicious sushi.

If you have catering trays and bowls that you can fit conveniently into your refrigerator onboard your truck or van, then you will have less food to move around when you arrive. Make sure you have enough trays, bowls, lids, covers, and wrap to cover foods you plan to transport. Air Pots® with handles are good for carrying coffee. Make sure you have insulated food carriers to keep food cold or warm as necessary. And before transport, make sure you have everything you need, from the foods to the napkins, toothpicks, and corkscrews. Make a transport checklist and follow it closely. Not having something on hand that you need is embarrassing.

> ## Smart Tip
> Transport food in insulated or electrically heated/cooled food carriers in order to keep foods at a safe temperature. Remember that foods should not be kept between 40 and 140 degrees. Make sure to follow all health regulations for your state when preparing and transporting foods.

For hot foods, make sure to have them heated and ready to go according to your schedule. Microwaves in your vehicle come in handy for some foods and burners at the party or event for others. Ask in advance if the location has a kitchen where you can heat up foods.

In many instances you will simply be asked to drop off platters and not serve. In such cases you need to have an abundance of disposable catering supplies at the ready. Here, your presentation of the foods on the tray can also score points. Good food plus a good presentation equals positive word of mouth.

Check out Food Service Warehouse at foodservicewarehouse.com/ for a host of disposable options. You might also check out Catering Supplies.com (cateringsupplies.com) or A S Catering Supplies, Ltd. (ascateringsupplies.com). Look for recyclable paper goods if possible.

Catering from Your Vehicle

If you are promoting your vehicle to be parked at parties or local events, such as a corporate picnic, you have home field advantage because you are working in or around the friendly confines of your truck or cart. Knowing what foods the client wants, what hours you are serving, and who is paying are the key concerns. If, for example, you are asked for 300 hot dogs, 200 burgers, and 400 cans of soda, you need to be paid accordingly for the foods plus your time.

Typically you should not be collecting money from the guests unless such terms are established in advance. Logistics is often an important issue. Campgrounds or parks require that you have a permit to park on the specific location. If you do these types of events often, check with the local parks department in advance. Parks are also very strict about where barbeques can be held. Make sure you are in accordance with the park regulations as well as those set forth by the fire department. The people planning the event should handle this, but often they do not. Don't leave it up to them, double-check and/or take matters into your own hands.

If you are asked to park on private property, make sure it is the client's property or she has written permission in advance for you to park there. Make sure you visit the site ahead of time. Stories of trucks that could not get down park roads or were too wide to make it over a small bridge are funny later on, but were not when the caterer tried to get to the party. Check out exactly where you are going and where you are parking.

Specialty Services

You can handle the food only or offer specialty services yourself or in conjunction with other vendors. Providing decorations, entertainers, or other party enhancements can bring in extra income while expanding your network. It can also be an extra headache when trying to arrange for a pony ride in a luxury-housing complex. Be careful what you promise. Of course, those same entertainers that you bring to a catered party can recommend your services to other people they know. Likewise, you can advertise on each other's brochures, fliers, and websites.

Specialty services, however, can also mean finding a special item for the birthday boy or supplying the cake. Sometimes this extra touch can make you the favored caterer in a community. Even bringing a gift for the birthday boy or a set of golden candleholders for the anniversary couple can be a special something that sets you apart from your competition.

The All-Important Costs

Every successful business needs to go from the red to the black by acquiring green. Yes, making money is what differentiates a business from a hobby. And while a mobile food vehicle or mobile catering business would be an expensive hobby, it is not that costly as a business. In fact, one of the reasons food-loving entrepreneurs take this route is to avoid the higher overhead of a restaurant although some may decide to go that route later on after proving themselves and building a following in the mobile food world.

Dollars and Sense

Sure, planning the menu and designing the truck are fun aspects of the business. However, culinary skills and creativity not withstanding, any food business, is just that—a business. Zach Brooks, founder and owner of Midtownlunch.com, a website which features the whereabouts of food trucks in New York, Los Angeles, and other cities along with other $10-and-under locales for lunch, says it's the same as starting a restaurant, the only difference is you're on wheels and you have a low overhead. "If you're getting into this business because you think you're going to get rich or be part of the new hot trend, don't do it," says Brooks, adding that it's a lot of hard work and the payoff is not usually that great for 12 hour days. "But, if the idea of driving a truck around, serving your own foods, being a part of that street culture, and making an okay living while doing what you enjoy sounds good, then by all means do it," he adds.

While foodies are turning the Food Network chefs and some of the hottest truck owners into major stars, the majority of entrepreneurs in the industry work long and hard without getting famous. Some are finding themselves in newspaper or magazine articles, or in blogs, while others are growing a major fan base on Twitter. Nonetheless, the hard work remains and the bottom line is still about making money.

To succeed in the business, you need to become cost savvy. "You learn about spending and saving money as you work in the industry," says Marcus Gotay, kitchen manager of WHEDco's four commercial kitchens in New York City, three of which are rented to the public on a regular basis. "You take inventory and see where you are spending money on a weekly or monthly basis and where you can spend more or cut back."

There's no set formula, but as in any business, especially when dealing with the food possibilities, you need to know what you are spending on the product(s) you sell, whether it's a cookie, an empanada, or a steak. You don't have to pay rent like a brick-and-mortar business, but you do have vehicle maintenance, kiosk space rental, parking permits, and other costs that need to be factored into the equation.

Obviously if you are selling a prepackaged item, it will be much easier to keep your costs

> **Beware!**
> One fact that many food cart and truck owners need to be careful about is the cost of parking their vehicle. Looking for lower rental (yet health department approved) overnight parking can be a big plus. With charges of $200 plus per month, parking costs can eat away at profits very quickly.

in line. But for those of you who are cooking your own food, it's a little trickier. When you add up your ingredients, packaging, marketing, logo, and all the other ongoing expenses and divide by the number of products or portions that you can sell in a given day, week, month or year, the question will be: Are you making a profit.

One former high-end cookie caterer realized, after three years of losing money, that it was costing $75 per cookie to run the business. That was reason enough to shut down. On the other hand, Celine Legros, owner and chef behind Les Caneles de Celine, a French pastry mobile caterer in New York City, calculated the costs of her ingredients, commercial kitchen rental, packaging, shipping, and everything else she spent on the business to determine that she was spending only $.17 per pastry. Therefore, if she sold a pastry at three times her cost or $.50 each, she would make $.33 per pastry. Therefore 250 pastries for a catered party would cost her $42.50 to make, and she would charge $125, or perhaps $100 at a bulk discount rate. Of course, if her competitors were selling French Pastries at $89 for 250, she might have to take a slightly lower markup—or prove that hers are worthy of the higher price.

The point is, you need to look very carefully at the type(s) of foods you are making, the cost of ingredients (including the cost of traveling to get ingredients or having them shipped to you), and all other factors involved in preparing your foods so you don't end up with a $75 cookie.

Business Startup Costs

There's no set formula for determining how much it costs to start a business. The field is broad, and there are too many possibilities. Clearly, a cart will typically cost less than a truck, and a prepackaged product such as ice cream, candy, or cans of soda are typically cheaper than making your own foods or beverages.

For your purposes, you want to make a list of each of everything you need from the truck, cart, van, kiosk, bus, and retrofitted equipment to marketing and promotion costs and home office equipment. The worksheet on page 116 is for you to fill in your rough numbers.

The range of costs varies greatly. You might spend $3,000 on a food cart, $500 on your initial food bill, $400 on permits and registrations, $200 on marketing, $300 on an attorney, and $300 for the first month to park and clean the cart. Tack on $300 in other miscellaneous costs, and you're off and running for $5,000.

On the other hand, you could spend $60,000 on a retrofitted food truck, $1,000 on initial ingredients, $2,000 on permits and licenses, $2,000 for the first month of a commercial kitchen rental, $300 for the first month of parking and maintaining the truck, $1,700 on kitchen supplies, $3,000 on marketing and promotion, $2,000

Sample Cost Worksheet

Your costs will vary according to the type of food operation, so add in other costs as they pertain to starting up your particular business.

Startup Costs

Cart purchase	$
Retrofitting (the cart may already meet your needs/specifications)	
All permits and licensing	
Cooking supplies	
Market research	
Website design	
Menu design and printing (include menu boards, handouts, etc.)	
Initial advertising and marketing	
Initial food purchase	
Initial paper and soft goods purchase	
Insurance	
Bookkeeping (ledger and/or computer program)	
Credit card processing capabilities	
Initial parking rental or deposit	
Initial commercial kitchen rental or deposit	
Accounting and legal fees	
Miscellaneous	
Total Startup Cost	$

on packaging, $1,000 to set up a small home office for bookkeeping, and $500 in miscellaneous costs for a grand total of just under $75,000.

Compared to a restaurant, even $75,000 is not bad for starting a business. The point is, it varies greatly. You need to do the math before spending any money so that you do not run out before you get started.

The numbers will also vary depending on your needs. Do you need an oven? A rotisserie? Coffee pots? A grill? Hot dog roller? The costs can range dramatically. Then, of course, you need to get and pay for all of the permits for the city/town you operate in, and board of health approval. There simply is no exact number, but you can be pretty sure the vehicle is your most expensive investment.

"For a beginner chef who wants to be an entrepreneur, or a chef who wants to downsize and make his life simple but still do what he loves to do, [a food truck] is a dream come true! This concept is simple and it's all about the net profit, not the gross! It is just a fraction of the cost of starting a restaurant," says acclaimed Chef Biagio of Milford, Connecticut's GotChef gourmet food truck.

Insurance Needs

Among the most important costs you will have is insurance. You need to cover both a business and a vehicle against as many potential risks as possible, especially if you are driving around with a few propane tanks strapped to your cart or truck. You need both liability and theft insurance. Review all other possibilities carefully, including those required by your state. You might even consider employment interruption insurance in case a natural disaster makes it impossible to do business.

Dollar Stretcher

Because a home office is not essential for this business, simply find a place in your home to quietly do the books and handle the payroll. And if you need some office equipment or furniture, look for used items or convert other furnishings into what you need.

Legal and Financial

Don't forget to set aside fees for an attorney and an accountant or bookkeeper to help you get your books set up. In all businesses, legal assistance and proper bookkeeping are vital. A business attorney will help you with contracts, setting up a business structure (LLC, corporation, etc.), and making sure you have met your business licensing requirements. Your accountant will set you up to handle local, state, and federal taxes as well as let you know what do and do not count as business expenses. Hint: save your receipts when you buy anything for the business.

Operating Costs

Your operating costs are the expenses you pay regularly to keep your business up and running. Consider these as the monthly payments, although some will be made weekly. Your operating costs will be both fixed and variable. Fixed expenses are those you will pay every month, such as:

- Vehicle payments (unless you've purchased your vehicle outright)
- Vehicle rental
- Commercial kitchen rental (This may vary depending on the deal you sign and the frequency of use: caterers often start with more open-ended deals.)
- Vehicle parking expenses (or space rental expenses for a kiosk)
- Insurance

Variable expenses are those that will change with the flow and/or growth of the business. Variable expenses include:

- Food and/or ingredients
- Parking permits (such as for special events or corporate parties)
- Delivery or shipping (this can change depending on volume)
- Gas and oil
- Vehicle repairs
- Packaging, labels, etc.
- Marketing and promotion
- Miscellaneous (including parking tickets, which you should try to minimize to keep the law on your side)

Numerous factors including the weather (which may preclude you from outdoor selling in places like New England or Minnesota in January or February) as well as peak tourist seasons and changes in parking rules and fees will factor into the variability of your costs.

You need to estimate how much you need per month, which means doing some math. Expenses such as food need to be watched the most carefully. Add up your weekly bills, and then calculate your monthly food costs (at 4.3 weeks per month). Do the same with paper goods or anything you are buying on a weekly or frequent basis. Monthly bills are easy. However, variables such as marketing and promotion are tricky.

If, for example, you need $1,200 to promote yourself at two fairs and you need to pay the bills in March and September (at $600 each), those are spikes for those months that do not fall into your usual pattern. You'll want to know which months are more likely to have higher totals than others. This can help you plan in advance. If, however, you buy a piece of new equipment in June for $1,200, for tax purposes you may wish to amortize the expense of the equipment over the year, which would be $100 per month for 12 months. Discuss the advantages of this with your accountant.

Growing Pains

Rome wasn't built in a day, nor was the success of the Kogi BBQ Truck in Los Angeles. Businesses endure growing pains. Zack Brooks notes that it takes time to make a go of it in the industry, whether you are running a cart or a restaurant. "You need to have enough capital on hand to last at least six months to a year because it takes time to become profitable. The most successful trucks are the ones that have been doing it the longest."

The rule of thumb, in business, says that it takes most new businesses at least a couple of years to show a profit. The larger the investment in the business, the longer it may take. Having a lower overhead, you can cut this number down by developing a good working business model. This means a business model whereby you have carefully thought about every step of the business process so that you can streamline it to be cost effective and time efficient.

Volume

One of the key factors in the food industry is volume. First, this refers to how much you buy, and then how much you prepare and/or cook during your time in the kitchen. It also refers to how much you can sell during your sales hours. Unless you are a caterer being paid in advance for X number of ice cream cones, chicken enchiladas, or steaks, you have a limited amount of time during your business day to sell your inventory.

Natasha Usher, who runs the Lucinda Creperie truck in Jersey City, New Jersey, also notes the importance of being prepared because your sales window of opportunity is limited. "We have lunch and dinner times, which gives us only about five or six hours in which to sell, unlike a restaurant where people can wander in at any time, so you have to be all prepared for those times of day," she says. But she puts in ten hours a day of work when considering the preparation, travel time, and cleanup.

Because many foods do not keep well overnight, you typically need to sell what you bring—and bring as much as you can sell. The Catch 22 is that knowing how much to bring is dependant on how much you can sell, and you don't know that until you sell out. Even then, you don't know how much more you could have sold. "In the beginning a lot of this is trial and error," says Marcus Gotay of WHEDco, adding that after a while you get a feel for it and it becomes easier to judge.

Volume also depends on the foods that you sell. That's why hot dogs, kebobs, ice cream, tacos, enchiladas, pretzels, cookies, cupcakes, and similar foods have been favorites of food vendors for years. They are easy to carry in volume, keep warm or cool, and sell quickly. They are also tangible. It's easier to say "I sold 62 donuts today" than to figure out portion size. It is, for example, harder to calculate how much pasta you can and will serve in a day (and less easy to manage), which probably explains why you see very few spaghetti trucks.

> **Tip...**
>
> ### Smart Tip
> Some cart owners have a second licensed cart ready to take over for the first one should they run out of food. This can continue the flow of service, but you'll need to pay someone to get that second cart to your location. Make sure the profits outweigh the salary of your assistant.

"You need to serve quickly in order to make your money," adds Natasha from Lucinda's Creperie truck. "Unlike a restaurant, your time frame is limited, so you need to make the most out of key times, such as 11:30 to 1:30, the lunch hours," says Brooks, regarding selling in volume.

While caterers typically accept credit and debit cards as well as personal checks, the mobile food industry operates primarily in cash. On the positive side, this speeds up the process. On the negative side, you do not want to be carrying around a lot of cash, especially at night. Cart and truck owners have reported robberies. It is, therefore, important to have someone working with you, or whom you know and trust, do a bank run during the day to get some of the cash out of the vehicle.

Pricing

It all comes down to pricing! If your prices are too high, people will not buy your foods. If your prices are too low, you won't make any money. So establishing your price is extremely important. Many people in business learn the hard way, by losing money for a while before adjusting their prices.

Zach Brooks and his midtownlunch.com website look for lunches valued at $10 or under. With the exception of some of the gourmet food trucks crossing the line and going up to $12 with specialty dishes, most mobile foods are priced at $10 or under. "Everything on our menu is $6 or under," adds Natasha Usher who agrees that you need to keep the prices down to build a following on a food truck. For catering, pricing is a different animal.

Pricing Principals

There are several factors to consider when determining your prices. For most familiar items, there are certain price points that customers will pay. You can typically get an idea of what they are by looking at various menus and doing some research. For example, a food cart or truck taco usually sells between $3 and $6, so you'll want to be within that range. Likewise, nobody is going to pay $6 for a water bottle (unless they are at a sports arena). The difference between charging $3 and $6 depends on a variety of factors, starting with whether or not you will see a profit when you factor in all of your costs. Below are some of the other determining factors, when it comes to pricing.

What a Customer Will Pay

What customers will pay is largely based on location and product demand. Someone in New York City will be accustomed to paying more for lunch than a person in Milwaukee. The affluence of a community and the lifestyle of the area(s) in which you serve both influence how much someone will pay for food. Some customers simply have more expensive tastes (literally), while others are on a tight budget and are more price conscious. The majority are willing to pay somewhere in between the common price points. Get to know which customers you will be serving.

Competitive Pricing

Take a look at what your competitors, or future competitors, are charging. Read various menus, particularly those posting foods you plan to serve. Make comparisons among like products. For example, compare chocolate chip cookies to chocolate chip cookies and not to oatmeal raisin cookies. Also look at portion sizes. If you've got the longer hot dog, you can charge more—yes, size matters.

You want to be competitively priced, which brings us back to those earlier price points. Of course, if you can price yourself below your competitors and still make a profit, that's great. If you are priced the same, then you need to wow customers with your food, your customer service, sense of community, or whatever else you've got above and beyond your competitors. Your advantage may simply be some good write-ups in the media or some great responses to your food on Twitter or Facebook.

Higher or Prestige Pricing

If you are charging more than that in the common price range, you need to have a reason why. It might be that you are selling homemade, organic products while your competitor is selling a commercial brand. You can then promote your competitive edge and justify your prices based on having the organic, healthier product. Reasons for charging a little more also include:

- Special ingredients or unique combinations
- Fresh organic or farm-to-table ingredients
- Sides, such as chips with a sandwich
- Portion size, more for your money
- Convenience (If the next closest sushi cart or restaurant is a mile away, customers might not mind paying a little more.)

Your Profit Margin

It doesn't matter what kind of pricing system you use, if you are not making more money than you are spending, you will have to make adjustments. You may need to find suppliers with lower prices. You may need to buy in greater volume. This might mean starting a food co-op to bring the volume of food up and the prices down.

Buying is a major factor in pricing in the food industry. That is why restaurant owners, and mobile food vendors, like you, shop at places like Restaurant Depot (restaurantdepot.com) or Jetro (jetro.com).

Many people in the food business also find certain items that they buy from unique suppliers that add something special to a key menu item. For example, pastry caterer Celine, who started and owns Les Coneles de Celine, does most of her shopping at familiar locations such as Costco. However, she buys specially made imported butter from France, and that is what distinguishes her pastries from those of her competition.

Caterers also need to determine the markup on their menu items largely based on their food costs as well as the cost of labor. In addition, they need to determine their costs for different-sized parties because prices when ordering vary based on volume and the number of employees will also vary. Using a tiered pricing structure, you can calculate the cost for different sized events. For example, the same party for 30 people might cost less per person for 60 people because you will not pay twice as much for the food. However, you may then need to factor in the cost of a second server because typically you look for one server per 30 or 40 people. If, however, you are delivering but not serving the food, the cost should be less then having a server included. Unlike a food truck, where a taco is on the menu for $5, your costs can vary depending on additional factors. For example, with a server a dozen tacos may come to $5 each. Three dozen may bring your cost down to $4 each. Without factoring in a server, three dozen may be $3 each. Shrimp filling might bring the cost up to $6.50 each.

While these are random numbers, they illustrate how a caterer has to price the same item based on quantity, having a server, and other factors.

Making Money

In the end, once you have determined your costs, you need to consider how many cookies, crepes, tacos, or portions you need to sell to overcome your list of expenses. Therefore if your total monthly expenses average $3,000, you need to sell more than 600 tacos priced at $5 each per month to break even, or roughly 140 per week or 23 per day if you work six days a week. If you average selling 50 tacos a day, or bring in $250 a day, you will make $1,500 a week or roughly $6,450 per month for a profit of $3,450 after expenses or $41,000 plus per year. Of course, this doesn't factor in the $10,000 you spent the first year on your truck or the $10,000 in additional startup costs. Remember, that first year is the toughest in which to turn a profit. Some vehicle owners report $200 a day in sales and others claim $1,500 per day. It depends on factors such as your location, your food, your marketing, your pricing, and your reputation.

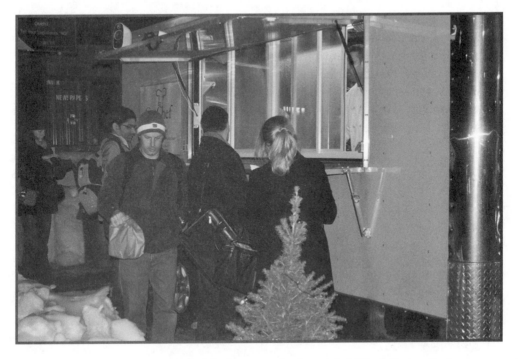

Holiday season sales are brisk at Got Chef gourmet food truck in Milford, Connecticut.

The night crowd gathers at the Streetza Pizza truck in Milwaukee, Wisconsin.

Of course, you may lose days, weeks, or even months in bad weather areas. Conversely, you may make up for this by taking on some catering jobs or selling products wholesale. As with any business, there are many factors that determine your success or failure. Some will be out of your control, but a lot will depend on your decisions and in this business your flexibility. Be ready to change your prices if you are losing money. However, if you are breaking even or making some profits in the beginning, have patience. Businesses need time to grow.

Finding Funding

For decades, many immigrants trying to make money in a new homeland poured their hearts, souls, and savings into their food carts. Whether it was on the Lower East Side of Manhattan or along Coney Island, where hot dog vendors dotted the boardwalk, it was a means to an end, a way of making a living. Today, entrepreneurs are thinking big and looking for financial backers to help them in reaching their dreams of success in the mobile food industry.

First Do the Math

Once you have reviewed your startup costs and ongoing costs, as discussed in the previous chapter, you can determine what size business to start and how much financing you will need. If, for example, you have determined that all of your startup costs come to $23,000 (including the first month's expenses) and that your ongoing monthly costs are $3,000, you'll want at least five more months (six months total) costs on hand to get started. Thus you would need $38,000 to keep you afloat for six months if sales are not good initially ($23,000 + [5 months x 3,000 = $15,000] = $38,000). You might decide to seek $45,000 in financing to have some cash on hand. Cash flow is vital to any business. Always making sure to have some accessible cash is important, especially in a largely cash business.

Your business plan will explain how you plan to sell enough enchiladas to cover your monthly expenditure. You can outline your costs and your potential profits on an Excel spreadsheet and work with the numbers until you figure out a price at which you can realistically come out ahead. Of course your startup costs will disappear after the first year (unless you are paying off a vehicle over time), but remember, a realistic forecast for making a profit may take at least one year.

Natasha Usher says $400 is a good day for her Creperie truck in Jersey City. In Manhattan, where the monthly costs of operation might be three times higher, some cart owners are pulling in $1,500 a day. The cost of living varies from city to city as will the cost of doing business and your potential income. Of course no business is a sure thing.

Once you have punched the numbers and assuming you can find decent, yet not spectacular locations, you can determine how much you may need in outside funding to get you started.

Funding

If you are looking for financing, even from friends and family, you should have a completed business plan with the financial pages included. A profit and loss statement projecting your profits over one, three, and five years (hopefully showing growth) can provide an idea of how you see the business becoming more profitable over time. Beyond the numbers, you need to explain how your system and your plans will build your revenue. What do you envision for the future? Be realistic, but have plans to expand your menu, increase your base of locations, do additional marketing, etc. Investors want to see the profit potential of a business and know that you have thought it through. That's why a business plan or at least a business summary is so important. Investors are more inclined to invest or lend you money if they see the plan on paper showing they can make a profit from investing or at least make their money back. After all, the age-old question from an investor remains: What's in it for me?

Sources for business funding include:

- Your personal savings
- Friends, neighbors, and relatives
- Assets
- Bank or credit unions loans
- Outside investors (including angels and venture capitalists)

Personal Savings

If you have money saved and set it aside for opening a business, you can determine if it is enough to start the business on your own.

If you have not been saving up specifically to open a business, you will need to prioritize your upcoming personal and family needs and then determine how much savings are left over after paying for necessities. Paying off debts is especially important before going into business.

It is not recommended that you dip into retirement savings or borrow against your credit cards, especially in a shaky economy. Savings used to start a business should be earmarked as such or so should money you can afford beyond paying off your debts and taking care of the needs of your family.

Friends and Relatives

Partnering and borrowing money are quite different. Dining has long been associated with families and today many food businesses, from restaurants to mobile food vehicles, are owned and operated by husband and wife teams or families. For instance, Van Leeuwen Artisan Ice Cream is owned by two brothers and the wife of one of the brothers.

Any kind of partnership needs a breakdown of responsibilities. If one person enjoys cooking while the other enjoys handling the marketing and production aspects of the business, then you are all set. Such partnerships, in which each person meets a different need, are typically the most successful. In all instances business papers should be drawn up to indicate who gets what if the family members go separate ways. Of course this is not always the case, and friction or bad blood is the result. Make sure to spell everything out in advance so you don't end up playing the blame game.

Many nonspousal partners also team up to run food businesses. In all cases partnership agreements should be drawn up with an attorney and signed. You'll be grateful later. It's important to spell out the specifics of the agreement. For example, one partner may be providing money but not taking part in the day-to-day operations of the business. Does she have a say in key business decisions? Is she a silent partner? Once you decide, put it into the agreement. Think of all the issue that may emerge and cover them in advance. If either partner feels that he will be resentful later on, speak up in advance and talk through the potential problems. The need for business partnership agreements cannot be overemphasized.

Beware!
Don't slice up the pie too many ways. Too many lenders can become confusing (as well as meddle-some). Try to borrow from as few people as possible.

Borrowing funding from a friend or relative is a different ballgame. Again, you need to draw up an agreement, but this should be a monetary agreement, meaning money is lent, to be repaid on a certain schedule or by a certain date, perhaps with interest. The biggest concern when borrowing money from friends or family is straining the relationship. Therefore, you need to treat such a loan as you would treat a bank loan and write out some terms about paying back the loan.

Seek people who believe in your business goals and will be supportive. Also seek people who will not expect that they have a controlling interest in how you run your business for their investment dollars.

Assets

If you already own a business, selling it or selling part of it can bring you some capital. If you do not need the money for bailing yourself out of debt or for other immediate needs, this is a great way to finance your new venture. Many new mobile food entrepreneurs sell off part of another business venture to buy their first cart or truck.

You may also have personal assets that you can part with to start up a new business, such as the antique car in your driveway or some old baseball cards worth $5,000.

Recently married couples have sold off one of their two homes once they began cohabitating, while others have rented out their old singles pad to bring in money.

Banks or Credit Unions

Banks, credit unions, and other lending institutions have long been the primary source for money for small businesses. If you are looking for business loans from commercial lenders, you need to have your financial matters in order. Commercial lenders want to know that you are a good risk.

A good credit rating is essential in order to demonstrate that you will be able to pay the loan back promptly. Before you start on your quest for money, it's a good idea to check on your credit score at the three major credit bureaus. Then you will know where you stand.

Do this just once because loan officers will also inquire and the more your credit ratings are checked, the more suspicious it often appears to lenders. Read your credit reports over very carefully, especially if your

> **Smart Tip**
>
> Contact at least one of the big three credit bureaus for your credit scores:
>
> 1. Equifax: 1-800-685-1111, PO Box 740241, Atlanta, GA 30374 (equifax.com)
> 2. Experian: 1-888-397-3742, PO Box 2002, Allen, TX 75013 (experian.com)
> 3. TransUnion: 1-800-888-4213, PO Box 2000, Chester, PA 19022 (transunion.com)

rating is not as good as you expected it to be. Credit bureaus make more mistakes than you would ever imagine. Make sure there are no errors on your credit reports. If there are errors, have them corrected.

It's important to get your credit scores in order before seeking a loan. You'll need to start paying off any and all outstanding debts and get to a point where you can open a new credit card or take out a small loan and pay it back promptly, showing you are on solid financial ground. Never go to places that can "magically repair bad credit." Remember, anything that seems too good to be true is usually a major risk. You are very likely to find yourself in a worse situation than you were in before.

Several factors come into play when obtaining a loan from a bank or a credit union. The economic climate, your track record in business, and your credit rating are most significant.

Lending institutions want to know that you are a sound credit risk. They will also want to know exactly what your future plans are beyond simply "opening a food business." This is where your detailed business plan comes in handy. Have people you know and trust look at your business plan to see that it makes sense. Your business experience should be included in your business plan. If it is not, make sure you highlight exactly what you have done before that makes you

> **Smart Tip**
>
> Always invest some of your own money into your business, even if you have to secretly borrow it from mom and pop. Lenders and outside investors look much more favorably on a business owner if he is "standing" there with them, taking the same risk. They figure that if you are willing to put your own money into this venture then you will stand behind it and take it much more seriously.

the ideal person to open such a business and run it successfully.

You need to put up collateral for the loan. Carefully consider assets that you can use for collateral. Avoid putting your home on the line. If you haven't run a business before, keep in mind that you can always start small on a shoestring budget from savings or loans from friends and/or family, then run the business for a short time before approaching a bank or credit union. This will show that you are seriously trying to make a go of the

Smart Tip

For information on starting and running a small business, as well as on market research and guarantees on business loans, check out the Small Business Administration (SBA) at sba.gov. Since 1953, the SBA has been helping entrepreneurs start, build, and run their small businesses.

business. People have started food carts for under $5,000 and run them successfully, showing profits. They have then asked for and received small loans to upgrade to a small truck or simply make improvements to the cart. Loans or getting a commercial line of credit can be used for business improvements. Spell out the need for and cost of the improvements you have in mind.

Outside Investors: Angels and Venture Capitalists

You may also look for outside investors to help you launch and even maintain your new business. Venture capital is the term for the money you are seeking. A well-constructed business plan and a good presentation are necessary to interest such investors. Because you, or you and your partner, are at the core of this business, the emphasis will be on what you have to offer in terms of experience, know-how, dedication, feel for business, marketing skills, and of course good food. It's not only what is on paper but also your presentation that needs to be polished. You want to be able to convey your passion for this endeavor and your commitment (remember, investing your own money is important) if you want to be taken seriously. You also need to be ready to answer all possible questions, politely and without hesitation. For example:

How long do you think it will it be before you will see a profit? Answer the question and have the paperwork ready, as discussed earlier, with your one-, three- and five-year projections.

Consider questions such as:

- If you are sick, who runs the cart?
- What locations have you determined are best for your truck?
- How much markup can you make per sale?

- (For a mobile caterer) Do you have a maximum order you can handle and what is that maximum?

The point is that for financial backing in any business you need to figure out all of the particulars in advance and be ready to answer whatever questions are asked with confidence. Hint: Don't ramble. Short answers with good explanations or specific examples will suffice.

The most significant concerns for investors are whether YOU can make this business happen and whether YOU are responsible, trustworthy, and able to run a team and sell a product. The more domain expertise you can show the better: Have you run a restaurant before? Have you sold anything to consumers as a vendor? Run a store? Run a food truck? You need to stand out because the business revolves around your vision.

"At GotChef, this was key. I had known the head chef, Biagio, for quite some time. He runs the number-one Zagat's and number-one open table-rated Italian restaurant in Connecticut. He runs an amazing restaurant and has a great reputation up here," notes Joe Rubin of FundingPost who helped GotChef get funded.

Also, consider what you are giving this investor in exchange for his capital. Remember, it's not a donation, it's an investment, a risky investment, and investors want to know what their upside is. How are they going to get their money back and then some! You need to know how you are set up to do this. Is it a profit share? Stock? Both? Work with your accountant and/or a business advisor in advance to determine the best way to repay investors.

Anyone could be a potential outside investor. However, if you are seeking more significant funding, such as $50,000 or $100,000, you may be looking for a venture capitalist or an angel investor. A venture capitalist is someone in the business of seeking investment opportunities, who provides capital for either a business startup or expansion. Typically, venture capitalists seek a higher rate of return than they would receive in other, more traditional, investments. They may be looking for upwards of 25 percent, which means that most small businesses do not go this route.

Angel investors, however, are people looking to back business ventures in hopes of making a profit down the road. Typically their expectations are not as high as venture

Smart Tip

Tip...

Develop your elevator pitch, a very concise pitch that defines your business idea briefly, explaining the business, the costs, your background, and why this business can work. An elevator pitch, typically 30 seconds, is designed to be told to a captive investor in the time it takes to ride up in an elevator. Near the end of the 1988 movie *Working Girl*, Melanie Griffith gives her pitch to the major investors in an elevator and wins them over by presenting a very sound and logical business proposal in roughly 30 seconds. That's how it's done.

capitalists. Many angel investors are busy working in their own fields or retired and seeking outside investments. In some cases an angel investor will provide expert advice, while in other cases she will serve as a silent backer.

Your Presentation: Make It Mouthwatering

The keys to your presentation to investors lie in the following questions:

- *Why is this a good idea?*

    Are you the first falafel truck in Portsmouth, New Hampshire? The only truck to sell homemade fresh ice cream in Seattle? The first truck to make Mexican food with a Korean twist and market it in largely Korean neighborhood? Are you the first mobile caterer to provide Hawaiian Luaus in office parks?

    The point is to illustrate what sets you apart from being just another business. Is it a great location, a unique menu, or perhaps the timing is right for your food to reach a certain demographic region. "Do plenty of market research," says Natasha from Lucinda's Creperie.

- *Who are you?*

    Just another person who wants to get into a hot business is not a good answer. Are you a great cook? (Bring food along.) Are you a great marketer? Do you both cook and market? Do you have a head for business? Are you great at managing the many details that go into such an endeavor? Are you a people person? Let investors learn to love you, but don't overdo it. Be yourself, not a character.

- *What makes your food so good?*

    Is it fresh from the farm? Homemade? Have a special "secret" ingredient? Food combinations never tasted before? Be honest and passionate about your food, but don't overdo it.

- *What is your marketing plan?*

    A few great locations? Promoting your catering company to party planners all over the city? Using Twitter and social media? Will you provide entertainment? The point is, let them know your plan for getting customers or clients.

> **Tip...**
>
> ## Smart Tip
>
> It's hard to find angel investors and/or venture capitalists. You might visit funding post.com, a business that arranges for special VC and Angel showcases in various parts of the country. You sign up and pay to attend such an event at which up-and-coming entrepreneurs, like you, get to meet with many angel investors and VCs in one place. Have your short elevator pitch ready and demonstrate the enthusiasm you have for your business venture.

- *What's in it for Me?*

  And remember, show them the money—or where it will come from in the end. Be realistic. and don't provide pie in the sky answers, even if you plan to open a Pie in the Sky food truck.

In the end, make sure you let backers or investors know where you plan to spend their money and be as transparent in business as possible. Transparency is a very popular term in business circles today. Basically, it means letting people know what you are up to and if something goes awry, acknowledging it and letting them know how you plan to fix any such problems before they become points of contention. Transparency builds trust, and trust builds a strong reputation in the business community.

11

Franchising

There are literally thousands of franchises in the United States, including many in the food industry. As the mobile food industry continues to thrive, more food franchises will provide entrepreneurs with additional business opportunities. The concept of franchising is based on a parent company, such as McDonald's or Subway, offering ownership of their business model to entrepreneurs in other parts of the country. The result is that entrepreneurs get to own and run a local business that is part of a large, typically successful, proven entity.

Perhaps the best-known franchised food trucks come from Mister Softee, which first showed up in 1956 with soft ice cream and frozen treats. Initially sold from ice cream stands, the company decided it could best reach more customers by taking its ice cream to the streets. So, with a catchy jingle to attract attention, off they went. Today, with more than 600 trucks and 350 franchise dealers, Mr. Softee is the largest franchiser of soft ice cream trucks in the United States.

The Pros and Cons of Franchising

Some entrepreneurs start looking for a franchise that sells a food or beverage of interest to them. Others seek opportunities based on the initial cost and requirements. Franchises, especially the most successful ones, usually make all of their requirements for becoming an owner (aka a franchisee) available.

The big plus of franchising is that you get name recognition. Starting a new business means having to establish yourself and build a brand from scratch. Having a well-known name can immediately draw customers. You also have a tried-and-true product, which means you can open more quickly, without having to go through the long process of creating and developing your food items. Buying a cart or kiosk of a well-known coffee company, for example, means you are selling a proven product from a company familiar to your target audience. Of course location will still be a factor in your success, but in many cases, such as with express food kiosks, the franchising company will have already done the research and scouted locations. In short, owning a franchise jumps you ahead in the process of opening a new business, letting you bypass much of the trial-and-error stage.

In addition, with sufficient support and guidance, as a franchisee you should not have to re-invent the wheel, so to speak, by doing everything yourself. Most franchises have working systems in place for running the business. As a result, franchise owners do not have to wait nearly as long to see a steady stream of income.

The biggest drawback to starting a franchise is the price. Franchise fees and overall investments can run to $100,000 and up, although some food carts can be much less. While you will see income more quickly, you may still be waiting for a profit because your initial startup cost is higher than starting up your own food cart or truck business. Also, before you start, there are financial requirements, such as total net worth and liquidity that you must meet. Then after you have started, franchises typically require you to pay royalties, perhaps 5 to 10 percent, of gross sales.

Another serious concern in buying a franchise is the franchise license agreement. It is imperative that you read and understand the entire contract. Having an attorney review it is strongly advised because there is usually a lot of fine print to decipher.

Another negative for some new business owners is the lack of freedom. You are essentially playing by someone else's rules. While you own the cart, kiosk, or truck, the franchise company has a say in how things are done. Therefore, if you want to be creative and march to your own drummer, franchising is not for you.

Buying a franchise lets you start a business more quickly and jump in with much of the preliminary work already done. It eliminates much of the risk of a brand new business and gives you name recognition and a tried-and-true product. Most franchises provide training and support, while many also offer financial assistance and payment plans. It is also easier to get funding for a franchise because of the proven business (of course you need to prove that you can run it).

Just remember that all of this comes at a higher price and will limit your creativity as you are in the business world not merely as an owner but also as part of a bigger business universe. So you do need to weigh the pros and cons carefully.

Finding a Franchise

It's not hard to find franchises, especially those making and serving food. However, considering the amount of well-known food franchises out there, you will not find a wealth of major food truck or cart franchises. Don't fret, this is a fertile market, and as established companies such as Sizzler, Johnny Rockets, and McDonald's, among others, take their food to the streets, such franchise opportunities are growing. Read about the food industry, especially the fast food companies and family restaurant chains, to see which ones are now looking into franchising trucks or carts. They may be the ones for you to explore.

There are a number of well-known food companies that are already franchising express-kiosks. You may have seen mall-sized kiosk versions of Baskin-Robbins or Ben and Jerry's. These are franchised.

To find franchise opportunities, you can start on the internet. Entrepreneur has an annual listing of the top 500 U.S. franchises. Many of the food businesses listed include express kiosks (entrepreneur.com/franchise500/index.html). Franchise Gator (franchisegator.com) and Franchise Finder (Findfranchise.com) are other websites that can help you look by industry or by state for franchise opportunities. They include information such as the liquid capital necessary and the total capital investment required. Sites such as these provide a way to narrow down the vast number of possibilities to a few based on your own criteria. You can also select a company, such as Mister Softee, go directly to its website, and look at Franchise Opportunities. For Mister Softee see mistersoftee.com/franchise-opportunities.

Franchise Brokers

When looking for a franchise, another option is to contact a franchise broker. As is the case with most industries, someone has come along to serve as the middle person to help you find a franchise opportunity. Such a broker can help you narrow down the possibilities and make a wise choice. The sheer volume of potential franchises is mind numbing. You've already narrowed down the field to the food industry and narrowed it down again to a kiosk or mobile business. Nonetheless, some individuals, as well as some parent companies, are more comfortable working through a franchise broker.

Beware!
While many franchisees are very happy with their agreements, some are not, due in part to the contracts and negative franchise provisions worked into such agreements. Visit the American Franchisee Association at franchisee.org, and click on Buying a Franchise to learn some of the worst franchise agreement provisions, along with some problems franchisees face. This is not meant to sour you on franchising, but simply to make you aware that some franchises are much better than others.

Brokers can find you various possibilities. However, keep in mind that brokers are working for specific franchises, so they are not necessarily impartial, looking out only for your best interests. If one franchise is offering the broker a higher commission for finding new owners then, not unlike some financial brokers, the franchise broker may steer you to the opportunity that provides him with a higher commission or a bonus. Therefore, get references before hiring a franchise broker.

Do Your Homework

You want to see which franchisers offer franchisees, like yourself, the best opportunity to own a successful business. Franchise owners have worked long and hard to build their name, recognition, and brand, so they are very protective and will restrict and control areas such as advertising and marketing, training, insurance, cleanliness, corporate image, the suppliers you may use, etc. This is their way of protecting themselves. Conversely, you need to protect yourself as some franchises can make life difficult for their own franchisees. For this reason, you want to check out a franchise thoroughly and talk to other franchisees.

You want to look for franchises that:

- Provide training and marketing
- Describe in detail what will and will not be provided by the franchise company
- Offer good financing terms
- Provide a detailed list of all fees that you will be charged
- Are transparent and provide sufficient company information
- Allow you to talk to other franchisees (this should be part of transparency)
- Offer clear dispute resolution procedures that are not markedly in favor of the franchiser (such as requiring you to attend arbitration hearings only in the state of the franchise company's headquarters)
- Offer you the same or a similar renewal contract (if they offer them at all)
- Provide an early-out provision in the contract if the franchiser/franchisee do not have a good working relationship
- Provide a clear and detailed procedure for you to sell or transfer ownership without having to waive your ownership rights to the franchiser
- Protect your territorial exclusivity

Eric Stite, founder and president of Franchise Business Review (franchisebusiness review.com), another good source for anyone interested in learning more about

---

Ten Things to Look for in a Franchise

1. A familiar franchise name and brand

2. Popular consumer products

3. A high-traffic location

4. Minimal labor requirements

5. Year-round sales continuity

6. Reasonable fees and commissions

7. Training

8. Ongoing support

9. A positive working relationship with the franchising company

10. A fair franchise agreement

▲

franchises, stresses the importance of talking to some franchisees before signing a franchise agreement. This can provide you with the inside track, letting you know how these business owners feel they have been treated.

Some Possibilities

A franchise owner of three Tasti D-Lite shops in Houston, Texas, bought a van for $90,000 complete with a small refrigerator, freezer, sinks, countertop, soft-serve machine, toppings bar, power generator, and a bubble-gum pink exterior that features the brand's logo and website address. Thus, he became the first franchisee to hit the road for the popular yogurt maker. More Tasti D-Lite mobile units may follow, as is the case with other corporate mobile as well as road versions of popular franchises. The question now is whether franchisers will sell a mobile franchise to an entrepreneur who does not also own an existing company franchise. Because the franchise truck concept remains relatively new for major companies, it is worth following closely.

While existing truck and cart owners may also be gearing up for franchising, some are already setting the wheels in motion, so to speak. For example, the owners of the Calbi truck in Los Angeles completed the necessary franchise registration in California to become one of the first Los Angeles food trucks to offer its business to potential operators.

If you look at Entrepreneur's Food Franchise category (www.entrepreneur.com/franchises/food/indexfood.html), you'll find many express kiosk possibilities available from well-known companies. The listings for these companies (and others) include a total investment range and franchise fees for a brick-and-mortar location, so you will need to inquire with the company regarding its express-kiosk possibilities. Companies to consider include:

- Baskin-Robbins USA Co.
- The Bearclaw Coffee Co.
- Ben and Jerry's
- California Quivers (a fresh fruit ice company also franchising carts)
- Cinnabon
- Corporate Caterers Franchise LLC (a mobile corporate catering outfit)
- Dino's Gyros Franchise Co.
- Dippin' Dots Franchising
- Dunkin' Donuts
- Famous Famiglia (pizza)
- FreshBerry Natural Frozen Yogurt
- Froots (Smoothies, wraps, salads, soups, juices)

- Great American Cookies
- Indigos Fruit Smoothies
- Juice It Up! (Smoothies/juice bar)
- KFC Corp.
- LaMar's Donuts
- Long John Silver's Restaurants Inc. (Fish and chicken)
- MixStirs (Smoothies, protein shakes, wraps and , salads)
- Nathan's Famous Inc. (Hot dogs, hamburgers, etc.)
- Nestle Toll House Cafe by Chip
- Papa John's Int'l. Inc. (Pizza)
- Planet Smoothie
- Quiznos Sub
- Saint Cinnamon Bakery Ltd. (Canadian franchise)
- Squeeze Fresh Smoothies
- Subway
- Taco Bell Corp.
- We're Rolling Pretzel Company

These are just some companies that list the express/kiosk as a franchise possibility. Each one will have its own system in place and a franchise agreement spelling out the details, including the franchise fee, overall investment cost, etc.

Licensing: Adding Your Own Personal Touches

It's all up to the company, but some franchisers will let you add your own flavor to the décor, while others will be more strict. In some cases, licensing a name and brand from another company may be a better option. Licensing provides you with greater flexibility to run the business as you choose, within the general provisions of the license. Companies monitor the use of their name and brand, but are not involved in the actual day-to-day operations of the business. Typically their concern is centered on maintaining the value of the licensed brand, product, or service. The cost of licensing is significantly less than franchising. Unfortunately there are fewer licensing options available.

Naturally, there will be licensing agreements that are very transparent and appealing and others that do not provide the whole picture or all of the necessary help

Licensing: Here's How It's Done

Scott Baitinger and Steve Mai, partners who own the Streetza pizza truck in Milwaukee, have already licensed additional new trucks in Cleveland. As Baitinger and Mai describe it:

Our mission is to work together to realize better sales and customer experiences than you would ever think possible. Streetza takes advantage of four key advantages when deployed into a new market vs. doing something on your own.

1. *Low overhead.* We are not a franchise, we are partnering with you. You can choose to use our recipes, or simply stick with your existing recipes. We will help build an efficient and reliable truck for you through our partnership. The total overhead will be less than 25 percent of opening a traditional brick-and-mortar store, once the lack of rent in highly trafficked areas are figured in.

2. *We use people's predictable patterns to help you position Streetza in exactly the right place at the right time.* We do this in two different ways. Through common sense monitoring and city traffic counts, we'll know the areas that are busy at noon, 5 P.M., and midnight. The truck will be moved into the heaviest trafficked area constantly. And the tools we provide you will show exactly where potential customers are at every moment of the day.

3. *Food trucks are still hot.* People love them. But, we provide much more to love than simply food. We have a brand personality, which is timely and relevant. We teach you how to listen better, react quicker, and generate interesting stories which people will pass on to others. This is how we can say that Streetza will be popular long after the food truck craze is over. Streetza is not simply a pizza truck. It's the community's pizza truck. Through our storytelling and promoting others in the community we can guarantee that Streetza will remain top-of-mind. Always.

4. *Not only will the truck be agile, the menu will be, too.* We'll work with you to identify trends in the city as they happen, making sure you have the most interesting menu in the city at all times. We'll work to partner with other restaurants to create unheard of flavor profiles and pizzas, which will keep the same customers coming back over and over again.

Streetza also provides access to the vault, so to speak, with a wealth of knowledge on areas including; Marketing Strategy, Social Media Strategy, Sales Strategy, Sales Forecasts, Management Summary, Projected Cash Flow (6 Months), Projected Balance Sheet, and so on. Streetza also provides its website, e-mail, accounting system and even insurance, as well as on-site training and 24/7 support.

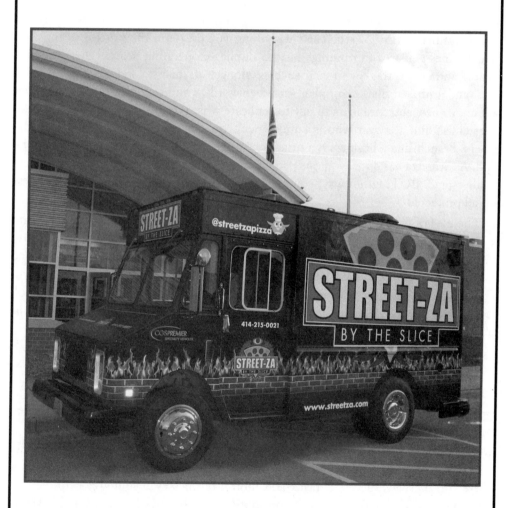

Soon there will be many Streetza trucks on the streets thanks to the owner's licensing plans.

and guidance that you require. As is the case with a franchise agreement, you'll need to read over a licensing agreement very closely with an attorney familiar with such business documents.

Franchising Your Business

You may be considering launching your own mobile food or catering business with hope of franchising in the future. To do so, you will need to establish a recognizable brand and make sure to trademark everything you create in the process of building your business. A smooth running, easy-to-duplicate operating process that you have created and own is the key to your success, along with quality food, a catchy name, a logo, and a proven marketing plan. In other words, you need a business model that will entice new entrepreneurs to pay to replicate what you are doing. This takes time to establish and a lawyer who is familiar with franchising contracts to draw up the papers. Franchising a business is a time-consuming process and your legal fees can be high. As Streetza has done, you can also license your model—the process is a little less cumbersome. BUT, either way, you need to have your concept, brand, and business model protected.

The idea of franchising or licensing your business is a marvelous long-range plan. It is something to strive for and requires you pay close attention to each step as you build your business. Write down exactly what you have done and how you have done it. Learn from mistakes you have made, and update your own business plan as you go. This way, once you have reached a point where your business is thriving, you can look back at how you reached your goal and market your knowledge, experience—and your brand—to others.

The Savvy Entrepreneur

One approach to building a business in conjunction with an established business is to take another brick-and-mortar business to the street. For this to work, you should have your business plan ready with one element to fill in, your menu items. This is where you approach successful brick-and-mortar businesses in your area with the idea of taking their food to the streets and promoting their business(es). Because food carts and trucks are the hot new trend, you'll want to arm yourself with a slew of articles about the industry, especially how popular it is in your area.

Such an arrangement could be beneficial for both parties. It supplies the foods and the popular name locally and eats some of your costs, while you find good locations where customers will eat their foods. Of course you have to work out a deal whereby you both make money. It can benefit the restaurant because your cart or truck serves as a billboard for its business and you are reaching new customers that it cannot get to by being a single location. Teaming up with a local food manufacturer can also work. EVOL Foods is doing this, designing trucks, going out with their own burritos, and serving them to people in order to increase brand awareness.

Having a cart at the ready may be the more cost-effective way to make this work, depending on the food in question. Your goal, however, is to introduce the idea, explain how you will be marketing a company's yogurt or ice cream, baked goods, or smoothies, and have its logo and signage. In essence, you become the mobile arm of the business for a fee and/or cut of what you sell. Having great locations in mind can make this work very well. Also, make sure you draft a contract that benefits both sides with a win-win agreement.

Such a plan to bring a business to the streets takes time to put together. You will need to show why you are the person for the job. However, with a bit of salesmanship, you can team with a business to launch its products and share in the costs of the operation.

Tip...

Smart Tip

If you take a mobile cart out for an up-and-coming company, find locations where its product is not yet on the shelves of local stores. This way you will not be competing with the local merchants. Have it in the contract that if the local merchant then sees your success and orders two-dozen boxes, essentially taking away your location, you get a cut because you helped make the deal happen.

Moving On

Michelle Lozuaway who, along with her husband Josh Lanahan, runs the Fresh Local food truck in Portsmouth, New Hampshire, have started considering selling the truck and moving on. Having a truck rated as one of the top ten food trucks in the country by *GQ* magazine, they are proud of their accomplishments. They brought street food to an area unfamiliar with the mostly urban phenomenon. The couple had already run a restaurant in Portsmouth and knew the lay of the land. So they bought a used 1986 truck, retrofitted it, and were off and running. "The truck paid for itself in one year, so it hasn't cost us anything more," says Michelle, who has enjoyed the food truck experience very much. Of course the fact that Josh was, and still is, a professional chef and Michelle took a cooking vacation in France helped the business succeed.

The couple loves their seacoast New England community and enjoys bringing street food to tourists and natives alike, but after losing battles to harsh winter weather, which does not help street food vendors in the northern states, they have decided to pursue a dream of opening a street food restaurant called STREET—Eat 360', which will be serving a host of interesting options such as Korean Fried Chicken or perhaps Porchetta sandwiches (Italian-style pulled pork) that are now served on the truck. "If the restaurant works as well as we think it will, we could use the truck to bring food to private parties," says Michelle, who has also considered selling it.

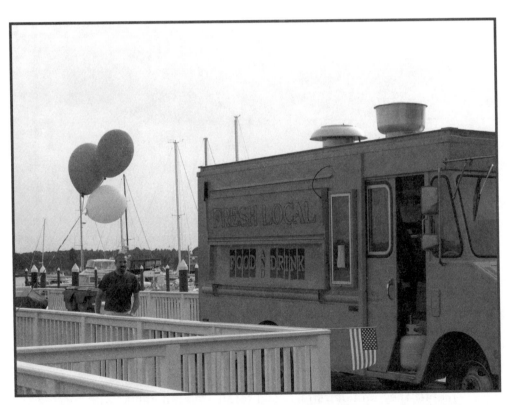

Wanna buy a truck? Michelle and Josh Lanahan may be putting the big orange Fresh Local truck up for sale.

"If we do decide to sell the truck, I want to see it go to a good home and be well used. It could do well anywhere they have more decent weather year round and a larger population. The truck is a gorgeous bright pumpkin orange, with big green letters that say Fresh Local," adds Michelle.

Selling a food truck, trailer, or cart is not uncommon, as evidenced by the many used models on the road today. There is a lot of work in running a mobile food operation, and people burn out. At that point they are either making enough money to hire others to run the show or they decide to sell the truck and move on. Those who have been successful often move into restaurants in some capacity, either as a chef, a partner in an existing venture, or like Michelle and Josh, as owners of a new eatery. Others sell the truck, buy a smaller van, and move to catering exclusively or to the food manufacturing business. Cody and Kristin Fields from Austin's Mmmpanadas truck are not yet selling their truck, but they have found a steady location where it stays on a full-time basis. They are now working to expand their growing wholesale empanadas business.

Selling Your Business

Selling a food cart, kiosk, truck, trailer, or even a bus is one possibility. The other option, if your business has built a following and/or established a brand, is selling the business. There is a difference, one is a vehicle (or kiosk) and the other is all that goes into the business. If, for example, the Big Gay Ice Cream Truck or the Kogi BBQ were to go up for sale as businesses, the buyers would be buying the entire culture, mystique, and business associated with the trucks.

If you have built a brand, you have to decide whether you want to sell the vehicle and maintain your business name, intellectual properties, brand, and so on or sell all of the above. This depends on your future plans. Certainly if you are taking your popular cupcake business to a larger truck or your famous fried chicken from a cart to a small storefront, you will want to keep your name, logo, and everything else and sell only the vehicle. If you choose to sell a vehicle, you can browse some among the many classified ads and compare your vehicle to other similar ones in your region. For example, you may see an ad such as:

4/27//2009 (Ann Arbor, Michigan) Homemade Ice Cream Trailer with 1997 GMC stock truck. Includes 20-gallon ice cream maker with 1923 JD 5hp hit and miss engine on a wagon, sliding glass door freezer, 2 door cooler, 21 cubic ft. Frigidaire chest freezer, folding canopy, 30" x 48"commercial grade wagon, two hole sinks, outside sink, water heater, backflow valve, electrical plugs, anything you might need to get started. Call Marvin at xxx-xxx-xxxx for more information.

If you were selling a similar vehicle, you could call Marvin to get an idea of the price to see if your selling price was in the same general area.

Among the many sites to visit, you can check out the ads on eBay under food trucks, or go to festivals-and-shows.com to find both used trucks and trailers. By searching the internet you will find other sites that post similar ads.

Getting a Proper Valuation

If you are selling your entire mobile food business, name, brand, logo, and customer base, you want to get a fair valuation. So you need to start planning well in advance. Selling a mobile food business is much like selling a restaurant, except location can vary depending on the new owner's preference.

You need to start by documenting how your business is run, from your ongoing cost of supplies and your other expenses through your weekly sales. You also have overnight parking, an off-site kitchen lease (if you need an off-site facility in your jurisdiction), and other things in place. These can be part of the deal, or not. The key is to prove the value of the business and have records for at least six months to show consistency. Nobody is going to buy a business based on a few good weeks.

Save receipts from your suppliers or vendors and copies of other expenses. Show sales totals for each day. Have your recent tweets from regular customers, and show the pages of the website. Illustrating that you have a loyal following can play a factor in the value of the business.

The truck itself also needs to be clean, and everything needs to be in top working condition. If you need to replace some older items, do so. It just like fixing up any vehicle for sale—having working parts counts!

It also helps to show that the business has been paying taxes and has been maintaining accurate books. Of course you should do this regardless of whether you are selling the business. You also want to show that you are not in debt. If you are paying off any equipment, let it be known if the buyer is picking up any debts you own.

An easy transition is also a plus when selling a business. The more you can make it a turn-key operation so that the new owners can step right in and get started quickly, the more appealing it will be to buyers who want to purchase an existing food business. After all, if your truck disappears from sight for a while, it will be much harder to pick up the momentum when the business returns to the streets.

If you have recipes written down and basic instructions as to how you run the daily operation, it can bode well for a new owner. However, you can also remind the new owners that they can put in their own touches as they see fit because it will be their business to run. When Natasha and Chris Usher purchased what is now Lucinda's Creperie in Jersey City, the truck was selling Mexican food. The owner sold them the truck complete with recipes and taught Natasha how to get it up and running immediately. While that worked fine for a while, Natasha was not happy selling foods that were not her own creation, so she switched to crepes. While she acknowledges that she might be making more money selling the popular Mexican food, she wanted to bring her crepes to the public and now has sales of 80 crepes a day, made fresh for each customer.

You need to determine how much you are selling, and if you get a fair price, it's time to let go, even if it means your marvelous meatballs will now be replaced by grilled cheese sandwiches. One good place to post is on http://us.businessesforsale. com. An ad for such a business, including truck and route, priced at $35,000 may look like this:

> Popular 1998 lunch truck with all the shelving, two freezers, storage and signage. Route included—16 regular locations—truck runs from 6:00 A.M. to 2:00 P.M. Two construction site stops alone bring in $200 a day each. Call now at . . .

While the idea of a mobile food business as a brand and not just a cart or truck is a rather new concept, the sale of a restaurant has been either a building and/or a business for years. Popular restaurants change ownerships but maintain the name and style that has built a lasting following. Less successful restaurants may sell the property, and let the new owner do as he or she pleases.

To sell, you will need to network and spread the word that the business is being put up for sale. From your followers to mobile food magazines and websites, you'll want to talk to people who actually get it and are part of the new street food culture. This helps you look for buyers who can appreciate the business and helps you advertise accordingly. Not unlike a restaurant sale, you should hire an attorney to work on the sales agreement. You also need to be patient.

Setting a Sales Price

First look at comparable vehicles of the same year and make as your cart, truck, or trailer to check prices. Then consider the condition of the vehicle as it relates to comparable vehicles. Then set your price up or down as you think reasonable.

Because it is not mobile, location counts for a kiosk. If you have an agreement with a location and a relationship with the mall or airport that your buyer can step into, that counts for something as well. If you are selling a franchised express-kiosk, you have to abide by the franchise agreement regarding a sale and work in conjunction with the franchise company or sell it back to them.

When pricing a business, your vehicle, other tangible items, and any intangibles such as a loyal following and popular brand are all used to set the price. After determining what your truck and equipment sell for, say $25,000, you need to measure the daily sales of your product. You will want to get a good estimate of how much of your sales are coming from regular customers. For example, if you can show that 20% your overall income, or $15,000, comes from regular customers, you

Beware!
Because many buyers cannot pay the full amount in cash, business sales often include the owner (you) getting part of the money up front and a note saying the buyer will pay the rest in regular payments. Make sure your note is legally binding (have a lawyer involved), and make sure the buyer puts up collateral of value (beyond the business assets) in case the buyer defaults on the loan.

will then want to add that to the sales price of your tangible assets. Therefore, if the tangibles, such as the truck and equipment, would sell for $25,000, you will add on the $15,000 that your regular customers will now bring to the new owner and ask for a sales price of $40,000.

All of this is what you need to calculate to come up with a valuation of your business. If you've worked long and hard at your recipes and at building up your following, don't sell yourself short. Some of the more popular food truck businesses today could easily sell for well over $100,000 because their brands are popular and customers seek them out. If that is you, all you need to do is prove how much business your truck brings in and what percentage is attributable to your brand, reputation, reviews, and the quality of your food—so keep good records.

If you own a catering business, your client list is your top asset. A truck is a truck, but the value of the list and the number of regular clients need to be calculated and sold accordingly because it would take a buyer much more time to compile a list of regular customers and a plan for the business than it would to simply find a van or truck.

Your recipes and kitchen skills are also part of the deal and need to be factored in. What is your value to the business, and how much is your knowledge and experience worth? This needs to be part of the equation. You also need to know the going rate for a kitchen space (if you own it) and try to gauge a fair price.

In any sale, remember to see how many potential buyers you get before selling. As is always the case, supply and demand count. The more in demand a catering business is in your area, the more money you can get.

Finding Buyers

Word of mouth and social media are two ways of spreading the word that you are selling your business. Because you are mobile, a sign on your vehicle can generate a buyer's attention. Classified ads and web advertising can also be effective.

Placing classified in newspapers or on websites is a very common means of making a sale. Because word count is typically limited, sum up the highlights of the business in a few key words. Provide phone and e-mail means of reaching you. Return calls promptly. Have answers at the ready for common questions, such as miles on the truck, equipment included, or the size of the van, or trailer. If people want to see what you are selling, meet them in a public place where you have room to park and talk—never let them take your truck for a spin unless you are sitting there with them and make sure they have a valid driver's license.

Smart Tip

Have someone with you to watch the buyers while you show them your van or truck. Believe it or not, opening up your truck to show someone around could lead to something being stolen.

Web advertising can be more costly, but placing a full-color ad on a website about the mobile food industry can be very effective. Again, be ready for callers or e-mails. In a web advertisement you can usually show a couple of photos as well as include more specific details about the equipment. Be accurate in whatever you write.

Staying Involved, or Not

If you are selling and moving on to other endeavors, you can make a smooth transition and be on your way once the business is sold. If, however, you want to remain involved you can include such a plan in the sales agreement that will have you remaining as chef or in some other role. This may not suit some buyers, but others may see the benefit of having you around to teach them the ropes. You have to work this out so you do not overstay your welcome. You also have to accept that you are no longer the boss but simply providing ideas or food. Another option is to stick around to simply help the new owner(s) through the transition period and then move on. Many former business owners see such a transition period as a means of closure.

And Finally

No matter whether you venture into the mobile food business with a part-time cart or a full-time bustaurant, there are a lot of factors that go into starting, running, and making a profit in this business. The most important things to remember are:

- Don't do this if you expect to get rich. Some mobile food entrepreneurs have made a bundle, but like most small businesses, the majority of owners work hard and get by.
- You need to do this because you enjoy providing people with good food.
- You need to wear many hats in this business from cook and server to marketer and promoter. Be as organized as possible.
- Don't get discouraged, even Kogi BBQ wasn't built in a day.
- Remember that being clean and sanitary are at the root of your success.
- Spend a lot of time doing research. From looking for the best vehicle to finding the best locations to watching the Food Network for tasty ideas, do all sorts of research. It's actually fun if you are into the food truck culture.
- Treat customers, food providers, competitors, health inspectors, police officers with tickets in hand, angry storeowners, and everyone else you encounter along the way with respect. It can pay off well in the end.
- Have a sense of humor.

Appendix
Food Truck Resources

They say you can never be rich enough or thin enough. While these could be argued, we believe you can never have enough resources. Therefore, we're giving you a wealth of sources to check into, check out, and harness for your own personal information blitz.

These sources are tidbits—ideas to get you started on your research. They are by no means the only sources out there, and they should not be taken as the ultimate answer. We have done our research, but businesses do tend to move, change, fold, and expand. As we have repeatedly stressed, do your homework. Get out there and start investigating!

Agencies and Business Associations

Small Business Administration (SBA)
6302 Fairview Road, Suite 300
Charlotte, NC 28210
Phone: 800-827-5722
Website: sba.gov

The U.S. Small Business Administration provides new entrepreneurs with a vast array of information on how to start and grow a business. It also has a business loans division that secures loans (but does not give them out). For more information on financing visit sba.gov/financing. To locate an SBA office in your region visit sba. gov/regions/states.html. You can also order the *U.S. SBA Small Business Startup Guide*.

United States Department of Labor
Office of Small Business Programs (OSBP)
200 Constitution Avenue NW, Room C-2318
Washington, DC 20210
Phone: 866-4-USA-DOL
Website: dol.gov/osbp
OSBP promotes opportunities for all kinds of small businesses, including small HUBZone businesses and businesses owned by service-disabled veterans.

United State Patents and Trademarks Office
Commissioner for Patents
PO Box 1450
Alexandria, VA 22313-1450
Phone: 800-786-9199
Website: uspto.gov

The Internal Revenue Service (IRS)
Assistance and information for individuals: 800-829-1040
Assistance and information for businesses: 800-829-4933
Website: irs.gov
All the tax information you could possibly want from the source. Forms and information about filing are also available.

U.S. Chamber of Commerce
1615 H Street NW
Washington, DC 20062-2000
Phone: 202-659-6000
Customer Service: 800-638-6582
Website: uschamber.com
The U.S. Chamber of Commerce represents small businesses, corporations, and trade associations from coast to coast.

National Business Association
PO Box 700728
Dallas, TX 75370
Phone: 800-456-0440

Website: nationalbusiness.org

A nonprofit association, the NBA can assist in helping small business owners team up to buy health plans, get educational opportunities, and secure other valuable services.

International Franchise Association (IFA)
1501 K Street NW, Suite 350
Washington, DC 20005
Phone: 202-628-8000
Website: franchise.org
An association with a comprehensive website about franchising for both franchisers and franchisees.

U.S. Department of Health and Human Services
200 Independence Avenue SW
Washington, DC 20201
Phone: Toll Free: 1-877-696-6775
Website: hhs.gov/ or foodsafety.gov/index.html
The food safety section provides a wealth of information on health issues.

Centers for Disease Control and Prevention
1600 Clifton Rd.
Atlanta, GA 30333
Phone: 800-232-4636, TTY: 888-232-6348
Website: cdc.gov
On the CDC website you can find a map leading to all state departments of health.

Southern California Mobile Food Vendors Association
Phone: 424-229-2874
Website: socalmfva.com
Plenty of information for LA area mobile food entrepreneurs and others.

National Restaurant Association
1200 17th St. NW
Washington, DC 20036
Phone: 202-331-5900
Website: restaurant.org
The mobile food industry is much like the restaurant business, only you have wheels and less overhead. You can find a lot of good information on a wide range of topics through the association's website.

National Association of Catering Executives
9891 Broken Land Parkway, Suite 301
Columbia, MD 21046
Phone: 410-290-5410

▲

Website: nace.net

The oldest and largest catering association in the world, it encompasses all aspects of the catering industry.

The American Beverage Association
1101 16th St. NW
Washington, DC 20036
Phone: 202-463-6732
Website: ameribev.org
Founded in 1919 as the American Bottlers of Carbonated Beverages, today the ABA represents hundreds of beverage producers, distributors, franchise companies, and support industries.

American Academy of Chefs
180 Center Place Way
St. Augustine, FL 32095
Phone: 904- 824-4468 or 800-624-9458
Website: acfchefs.org
Part of the American Culinary Foundation, founded in 1929, it now has 225 chapters nationwide. When it comes to cooking, it is the expert.

Cart, Truck, Kiosk, Trailer, and Bus Designers and Manufacturers

Most of these companies will help you meet health compliance regulations in your city or state. Although some have "cart" in the name, many also sell kiosks.

800 Buy Cart
800buycart.com

All A Cart Manufacturing
allacart.com

Airstream Trailers
airstreamtrailers.com

All Star Carts and Kiosks
allstarcarts.com

Apollo Carts
apollocarts.com

California Cart Builder
californiacartbuilder.com

Cart Concepts International
cartconcept.com

Cart King
cart-king.com

CateringTruck.com™
cateringtruck.com

Concession Trailers Warehouse
concessiontrailerswarehouse.com

Creative Mobile Systems
cmssystem.com

Festivals and Shows.com®
festivals-and-shows.com/catering-trucks-for-sale.html

Food Cart USA
foodcartusa.com

Food Trucks.org
foodtrucks.org

Ice-Cream-Trucks.com
ice-cream-trucks.com

Kitchens on Wheels®
rollingkitchens.com

Lunch Trucks 4 Sale
lunchtrucks4sale.com

M and R Custom Concession Trailers
mr-trailers.com/ConcessionTrailers

Magnolia Carts
magnoliacarts.com

Mobi Munch (food trucks)
mobimunch.com

Plano Sales East
cateringtrucksbyplano.com

▲

Roadstoves
roadstoves.com

Trovit (under cars section also has food lunch trucks)
cars.trovit.com/used-cars/lunch-catering-truck

Vending Trucks.com
vendingtrucks.com

West Coast Custom Carts
westcoastcustomcarts.net

WYSS Catering Truck Manufacturing
wysscateringtrucks.com

Vehicle Wraps

Advertising Vehicles.com
advertisingvehicles.com

Cliff Digital
cliffdigital.com

San Diego vehicle wraps
sandiegovehiclewraps.com

Commercial Kitchens for Rent or Lease

Biz Kitchen$
bizkitchens.com
Commercial kitchen postings and connections

Commercial Kitchens for Rent
commercialkitchenforrent.com
Kitchen rental state by state

Culinary Incubator Kitchens
culinaryincubator.com
Kitchen rental state by state

Chef's Kitchen (LA)
chefskitchens.com

Cookspace (Seattle)
206-283-6003

Kitchen Chicago
kitchenchicago.com

The Kitchen Space (Austin)
thekitchenspace.com

La Cocina (SF)
lacocinasf.org

WHEDco Kitchen Incubator (NY)
whedco.org/kitchenincubator.php

Equipment and Supplies

Barbeques Galore
bbqgalore.com

Business.com
business.com
Directories of manufacturing companies, websites, and articles in various categories
Search under the following headings: beverages, bustaurants, trucks, food, kitchen equipment, food carts, food kiosks, food trailers, or food trucks.

The Fire Within...
portablebrickpizzaoven.com (Portable pizza ovens)

Food Service Warehouse
foodservicewarehouse.com
Tons of equipment at your fingertips

Make Ice Cream.com
makeicecream.com
Ice cream making equipment

My Cleaning Products
mycleaningproducts.com
Natural cleaning products

Northern Pizza Equipment Inc.
northernpizzaequipment.com

Franchising

Entrepreneur Top 500 Franchises
entrepreneur.com/franchise500/index.html

Franchise Business Review
franchisebusinessreview.com
Comprehensive publication about franchising

Franchise Gator
franchisegator.com

International Franchise Association (IFA)
franchise.org

Funding

Funding Post
fundingpost.com
Runs venture capital and angel showcases nationwide where entrepreneurs can meet with VCs and angels to discuss funding new projects (such as your mobile food business)

Eco Business Links
ecobusinesslinks.com/green_venture_capital.htm.
Green business investors

Mobile Food Industry Information

Buzzle.com Food and Drink
buzzle.com/chapters/food-and-drink.asp
Food articles and plenty of recipes

Hotdog Cart Secrets
hotdogcartsecrets.com
All about owning a hot dog cart

Find LA Food Trucks
findlafoodtrucks.com
Locations plus blogs and other information about LA food trucks

Midtown Lunch
midtownlunch.com
Data about the mobile food business in several cities

Mobile Catering Business.com
mobilecateringbusiness.com
Links to articles, business plans, forums, books, and more

Mobile Food News

mobilefoodnews.com

News and information about the mobile food industry

New York Street Food

newyorkstreetfood.com

The latest updates on the NY street food scene

Sally's Place

sallybernstein.com/food/chefs-corner/organizations.htm

Includes a long listing of professional food organizations, articles, and more

National Food Suppliers and Food Clubs' Websites

BJs

bjs.com

Business.com

business.com (look at its food and beverage directory)

Cheney Brothers (South East)

cheneybrothers.com

Costco

costco.com

Food and Beverage Network

foodandbeverage-network.com.

Food Service.com

foodservice.com/foodshow/foodservice_distributors.cfm

Jetro

jetro.com

National Food Exchange

nationalfoodexchange.com

Natural Food Co-ops

coopdirectory.org

Performance Food Group

pfgc.com

▲

Convenience Foods

Restaurant Depot
restaurantdepot.com
For people in the restaurant and food business like you.

Sam's Club
samsclub.com

Smart and Final (West Coast)
smartandfinal.com

Sysco
sysco.com

United Natural Foods
unfi.com

US Foodservice
usfoodservice.com

Catering Supplies

Catering Supplies.com
cateringsupplies.com

A S Catering Supplies, Ltd.
ascateringsupplies.com.
Numerous supplies and a newsletter

Other Business Websites

Business Plans

Bplans.com
bplans.com
Expert advice, business planning tools, and sample business plans

BizPlanDB
bizplan.com
Online business plan software

Credit Bureaus

Equifax
   800-685-1111
   equifax.com

Experian
   888-397-3742
   experian.com

TransUnion
   transunion.com

Incorporation and Legal

The Company Corporation
   incorporate.com

Nolo.com
   nolo.com

USAGov.com
   usa.gov/Business/Incorporate.shtml
   U.S. government's official website included data on incorporating in all 50 states

Business Books

55 Surefire Food-Related Businesses You Can Start for Under $5000, Cheryl Kimball, Irvine, CA: Entrepreneur Press, 2009.

From Kitchen to Market: Selling Your Gourmet Food Specialty, Stephen Hall, Chicago: Kaplan Business, 2005.

Food Trucks: Dispatches and Recipes from the Best Kitchens on Wheels, Heather Shouse, Berkeley, CA: Ten Speed Press, 2011

How to Open a Financially Successful Bakery (with CD), Sharon Fullen and Douglas R. Brown, Ocala, FL: Atlantic Publishing Company, 2004.

Start Your Own Restaurant and Five Other Food Businesses, Jacquelyn Lynn, Irvine, CA: Entrepreneur Press, 2006.

Successful Business Planning in 30 Days: A Step-By-Step Guide for Writing a Business Plan and Starting Your Own Business, Third Edition, Peter J. Patsula, Arlington, TX: Patsula Media, 2004

Small Business Software

Business software can help you with bookkeeping, record keeping, vendor and supplier lists, paying taxes, etc.

Business Plan Pro and Palo Alto Software
  Marketing Plan Pro
  paloalto.com

Microsoft Office Small Business Accounting and Microsoft Office Small
  Business Management Edition 2006
  microsoft.com

QuickBooks Pro 2006
  quickbooks.Intuit.com

Quicken Deluxe 2011
  quicken.Intuit.com

Internet Business Resources

All Business
  allbusiness.com
Articles, information, tips, links, business forms, directories, expert commentary, etc.

Cafepress.com
  cafepress.com
Helps you sell gifts and promotional products from your website

Entrepreneur Online
  entrpreneur.com
Articles, information, tips, links, business forms, directories, expert commentary, etc.

Go Daddy
  godaddy.com
For building your website

MerchantExpress.com
  merchantexpress.com
Provides merchant accounts and credit card processing options and solutions

Network Solutions
 networksolutions.com
Helps you search for web names

Nolo.com
 nolo.com
Comprehensive legal site with listings of attorneys in your state, plus articles, legal forms, and much more

Thomas Register
 thomasnet.com
Helps you search for registered and unregistered trademark names

Additional Online Resources and Recipe Websites

Abouteating.com

Allfood.com

Allrecipes.com

Anoccasionalchocolate.com

Americastestkitchen.com

Bbc.co.uk/food/recipes

Bestfoods.com

Betterrecipes.com

BettyCrocker.com

Campbellsoup.com

CDkitchen.com

Chinavista.com/culture/cuisine/recipes.html

Cooking.com

Cookingcache.com

Cookingconnect.com (cooking appliance reviews)

Cooks.com

Coopdirectory.org

Culinarybusiness.com

Epicurious.com (recipes)

Farmersmarket.com

Food.com

Foodnetwork.com

Healthrecipes.com

Ihirechefs.com (chef hiring website)

KatenConsulting.com (food serving etiquette and training)

Mobilecravings.com (food truck index in many states)

Myrecipes.com

Onestopcandle.com (chocolate and candy-making supply company)

Recipes2.alastra.com

Recipetrove.com

Salsa-recipes.com

Thefruitpages.com

Whatscookingamerica.net

Whfoods.com

Glossary

Air Pot® beverage dispenser. A thermal beverage holder that uses vacuum insulation to keep contents hot or cold. It uses air to pump out the contents, so it is referred to as an "air" pot.

Background check. The process of looking up and compiling data on a potential employee, such as a criminal past or work-related inconsistencies with information provided.

Brand. The identity of a product, service, or business, which can include the name, logo, slogan, or anything else unique to the business.

Business plan. A detailed plan of how the business will be started, operated, and will show a profit. Business plans are divided into several sections and tell the story of the business particularly (but not exclusively) for potential financial backers.

Business summary. A short version of a business plan that tells the key points of how the business will operate and earn money.

Cold trays. Thermal trays that when heated work like a freezer to store cold foods or beverages.

Commercial kitchen. A kitchen owned and operated to be rented out commercially for use by others.

Commercial line of credit. Not unlike a credit card, it is a line of credit extended by a bank or credit bureau specifically to a business.

Commissary kitchen. Another name for a commercial kitchen.

Convection oven. An oven using a fan to shorten the cooking time by circulating hot air uniformly around the food.

Credit reports. A detailed report of an individual's credit history prepared by a credit bureau and used by a lender to determine a loan applicant's creditworthiness.

Credit union. A cooperative organization that makes loans to its members at low interest rates.

DBA (Doing Business As). Name used for business purposes that is not the legal name of the individual or organization actually conducting the business. The DBA is typically on file at the courthouse as a fictitious name by which you or your company does business.

Employer Identification Number or EIN (aka a federal tax ID). According to the IRS, it is also known as a Federal Tax Identification Number and is used to identify a business entity. Generally, businesses need an EIN.

Fire-suppression device. An automatic warning and shut-down device attached to an oven or stove to shut it down in the event of a fire.

Flattop grill. A grill resembling a griddle, except the heating element is circular rather than straight.

Foot traffic. Pedestrians who pass your location.

Franchise. An agreement between a company franchising its business model to business owners who agree to operate a business according to the rules and regulations of the franchising company.

Franchisee. The buyer/owner of an individual franchise or several franchises from a franchising company.

Franchisor. The company selling a franchise.

Gross vehicle weight. What a vehicle weighs at any given time.

Hood/commercial hood. A hood captures all contamination from grease and oil emanating from a stove or grill. It must be removed and cleaned periodically.

POS technology. Point-of-sale (POS) technology calculates items checked out using computer software.

Propane tank. A tank, often used on food trucks, that contains the colorless gas C3H8 (found in natural gas and petroleum) and widely used as a source of energy for onboard equipment.

Pushcarts. A light cart pushed by hand.

Retrofit. To remodel, design, and/or refurbish a cart, truck, trailer, kiosk, or bus to meet the needs of the owner.

Serving windows. The window on the side of the vehicle through which orders are taken and customers are served.

Social media. The various forms of online communication: blogs, microblogs such as Twitter, social networking sites such as Facebook, and iPhone or Blackberry applications.

Transparency. In business, it means making the systems, policies, operating procedures, and financial data (within reason) available to shareholders and the public.

Viral marketing. Online marketing that replicates word-of-mouth marketing. Viral refers to the speed of spreading the word (it is not a negative term such as a virus). Forwarding to a friend or a specific message at the end of a mass e-mail can be forms of viral marketing.

Zoning. A municipality's way of dividing up a territory (city, town, etc.) by commercial and residential areas.

Index